# The Life Map

A Guide to Writing the Blueprint for
Where You Want Your Life to Go

I0078764

## Colleen Blake-Miller

CONCLUSIO
HOUSE PUBLISHING

Printed in Canada

First Printing, 2014

ISBN 978-0-9938420-1-6

Conclusio House
Toronto, Ontario
Canada

# Dedication

*This book is dedicated to my boys Leroy Jr., Blake-Joshua, and Jeremiah-James. Let no one limit your potential, for with Christ all things are possible.*

# Acknowledgments

Thank you to my husband, Leroy, who is always encouraging and supporting my dreams. And to our little boys who bring laughter and joy into our lives daily.

To my parents who have encouraged me to pursue my passion for helping people. Thank you for your unconditional support.

To my big sister, Nadia, thank you for being a great role model who has showed me the right way to go on so many occasions, and to my brother who always comes through at the eleventh hour.

To my cousin, Katherine, who was the very first person who listened to me share my idea for *The Life Map*, and was willing to be the first person I practiced all my crazy ideas on.

To my editor and friend, Kerri-Ann, who reminded me, time and time again, that I would get my book completed and that it would be great.

And, finally, to all my family, friends, and clients who allow me to learn so much through their lives. Thank you all.

My prayer is that God would be pleased with this project, and that He above all else would get the glory for what is accomplished by it!

# Table of Contents

# Introduction

Walking through life without realizing your inner potential is no less than tragic. I've heard people say, "Oh, that young man/woman has so much potential," and I think to myself, "Who doesn't?"

Everyone has potential; we all have things inside us that were meant to be shared with the world—a dream, a goal, a purpose—something inside that needs to come out. No one is exempt, we've all got something we need to accomplish, we're all filled with potential.

Unfortunately though, for many, this potential is never manifested. The dreams don't get realized and the goals are never met. I'm sure that if surveyed, many people would offer their story as to why they were never able to accomplish their dreams.

What goes through your mind when you consider the fact that the potential you carry inside you could possibly go unrealized? Are you saddened? Are you concerned? Are you scared? Is this what you want for yourself? I hope your answer is a resounding "No!" and if not, you're reading the wrong book.

Figuring out how to make your dreams and aspirations come true is not always clear cut. How we envision our future typically comes quite easily; it's mapping out the steps to make those dreams a reality that usually leaves us confused.

## What is *The Life Map* all about?

*The Life Map* is designed to help you outline your sense of purpose, identify one thing you would like to focus on accomplishing, and make a plan to accomplish that goal. By the time you get through reading this book, you would have set some goals for your life, and would've developed a plan for how to achieve these goals by a specific end date.

The biggest, most important part of this book is to convey the message that if you want to see your life take a particular path, you can't just dream it, you can't just think it, you can't just hope and believe that it is going to happen, you have to be intentional. Realizing your life's goals requires making a plan and following it through to the end. Your map will lead you to your destination. *The Life Map* will help readers see that their lives have purpose, and remind them that they are not here by accident since a lot has gone into creating them. This is a book for effective planning that leads to success. It will build hope in all its readers and bring clarity in the area of vision realization.

The great thing for me is that I am not the one who will be bringing clarity or depositing ideas or even giving the hope. People will discover the clarity they have been seeking by answering the deep questions that have been strategically asked throughout the book. I am excited because everyone has the potential to really change their lives in a positive way. My prayer is that through this book you will experience a mind-shift that will allow you to begin to do things on purpose and be more intentional about what you do with your time. Time is a gift and a limited resource. Our days are numbered and, although we don't know when, they will eventually come to an end. This book will help you to consciously live out the life you desire with the time God has blessed you with.

Enjoy,

*CBM*

# Chapter 1
# Where Am I Going?

When you stop and consider your life, how often do you think about where you are going? Do you ever stop and think about your life, the path you are on, and where this path is leading you? It is easy to get so caught up with responsibilities and the routine hustle and bustle of daily life that we miss asking ourselves the very important question: "Where am I going?"

We are all headed somewhere in our lives, whether we stop to consider it or not. Each choice we make is a step that leads us down a path to a particular destination. At first glance, the title of this chapter may seem inane. But this is a question that only you can answer because you will have to take responsibility for where you end up. I like to challenge people to consider their final breath and what they would like to have accomplished by that point, then move backwards from that moment in the future to today. Essentially, you're saying, "Given what I want my end to look like, this is what I plan on doing with my today."

What is your purpose and what is your goal in life? These are tough questions to consider at times, but *The Life Map* will offer you a plan to help you accomplish both your purpose and your life goals. What are you here on this earth to accomplish? What do you want to ensure that you do before you take your last breath?

I believe that by allowing yourself to grapple with these questions you will move closer to understanding where you are going, because where you are going is determined by what you believe you are purposed to accomplish in your life. The goals you set for yourself are connected to the place you get to in life.

What comes to mind when you see the word *purpose*? One definition of the word purpose is 'the reason for which something is done or created or for which something exists.' With this definition of the word purpose in mind, how do you answer the question, "Why am I here?" Do you believe that life is a random course of events without rhyme or reason? Or do you believe that you were created on purpose for a purpose? Recognizing that there is a reason for our existence gives meaning to life and allows us to consider what it is that we do differently from someone who doesn't think there is purpose on their life.

It's possible to be on the journey of understanding your purpose, and that's fine. In that case, I would say that you could consider the question "What should I do with my life?" Consider your dreams, things that you are interested in, things you are passionate about, and also consider the things you're good at.

Considering what others think you are or could be good at is another way to help determine your purpose if you are having a hard time figuring it out. But it's important to remember that no one is going to force or make you fulfil your purpose, and you cannot rely on the ideas of other people alone or wait for others' permission to get your purpose accomplished.

> We are all headed somewhere in life.

It's important to have the support of family and friends who know you well; however, you may be faced with the opinions of people who doubt what you are pursuing. Part of maturing is learning how to hear negative opinions without letting them deter you from your course. You need to be relentless in pursuing your purpose. No one else is going to give 100% to your life like you would because no one is as invested in your success as you are.

Purpose is such a big subject that it couldn't possibly be covered and understood in just a few paragraphs. It is, however, something we all need since it gives us stability and security in life. Consider where you are right now. What has your life been like up to this point? How do you feel about how you've used your time thus far? Do you feel happy about your accomplishments? Or do you feel like you could have made better use of your time and talents? Do you feel disappointed with the time that's been wasted not accomplishing much? What things have you done in the past that you're proud of and want to continue doing? What are the things in life that you want to avoid doing again?

Having considered your purpose, fill in the following by writing your name in the first space and what you think your purpose is in the second space. _____'s purpose in life is to _____.

Are you able to confidently fill in the second space? This is a very important exercise and it deserves an honest attempt because not knowing your purpose can haunt you throughout your entire life.

My thoughts on purpose:

1. We all have one, whether we recognize it or not
2. Learning to fully understand and fulfil our purpose is a lifelong journey
3. There is a deep longing in each of us to fulfil this purpose
4. Our gifts and talents are ours to use in accomplishing our purpose
5. Life without a sense of purpose can be very meaningless and empty
6. Living out our purpose gives us a great sense of fulfillment

Consider the plans you have for your future. We are all headed somewhere in life. We are all in the midst of doing something; even doing nothing is essentially doing something. Now take some time to consider what you'd like to achieve in the future; are there any goals that you'd like to pursue? Is there something specific that you believe your future should include?

Purpose can be considered a compass because it helps us to make strategic choices in life and helps us avoid making the wrong choices that would lead us away from achieving our goal. For example, when a young adult has a sense of purpose or goal for her future, she will avoid those situations that could prevent her from attaining her future goal. Likewise, should she lack a sense of purpose in her life, she may not be as selective about the situations she gets involved in. The bottom line is that having a sense of purpose can affect the choices we make and can potentially change the trajectory of our lives.

Purpose can sometimes be hard to define and pin down. Understanding our purpose isn't something we discover and then move on from, never to discuss again. Instead, our understanding of our purpose continually grows throughout our lifetime. As we experience life, and as we mature and grow, our understanding of our purpose will evolve. Questions like 'Why am I here?' 'What am I supposed to be doing with my life?' and 'Why do I exist?' will generate different answers at different times in our lives. Hence, I believe that it is okay to be engaged in the ongoing conversation of 'Why am I here?' 'What's the point?' 'What am I supposed to be doing?' and so on.

Have you ever questioned your purpose? What are the experiences that have left you questioning what you were called to do? Regardless of how you feel, what you've been told, or what you've experienced, everyone has something to offer the world, a message to share, and something to bring to the table. Yet, oftentimes, our message isn't heard, our gift isn't received, and our purpose isn't fulfilled.

Some people don't ever fulfill their purpose because of self-doubt. Others don't fulfill their purpose because they are confused as to how to accomplish all of what's inside. And others just never follow-through on the things they know they need to do to get stuff done. Whatever the reason, the result is the same—missed opportunity, lost potential, lost purpose, and unfulfilled purpose.

Purpose is the reason for which something exists. Therefore, when we consider our own purpose we must consider the reason for which we exist. It's not an easy thing to figure out, but once you do, it begins to impact how you live your life, the choices you make, the things you say *yes* to, and the things you say *no* to.

Though we all have purpose, we don't all live out our purpose. If we aren't careful, we can walk through life filled with potential and promise, yet realizing little to none of it. If you don't make a plan for walking and living out your purpose, the chances are minimal that you'll actually realize all of your potential. Early on in life, lost opportunities may not be too discouraging; however, the older you get, the more depressing it is to look back and realize that you haven't utilized your potential the way you could have. Age has a way of putting missed opportunities into perspective.

It is an unfortunate reality, but there are too many people who live out their lives with a sense of confusion as it relates to accomplishing their hopes and dreams. Unmet dreams are difficult to bear, and purposelessness is no easier. Not knowing your purpose can seriously impact your sense of worth because it's easy to give in to thoughts that you don't matter in the world.

Three things to consider when determining your purpose are:

1. Your ultimate life purpose
2. Your gifts
3. Other passions and responsibilities

## Ultimate Purpose

When determining your ultimate purpose you must first consider your bottom line. What is the thing that you know you want to have done or accomplished by the time you take your last breath? Your ultimate goal is something that goes beyond you and something that will live on past your time here on earth.

According to the way society is progressing, it's very easy to become self-absorbed. But the truth is if you or I die tomorrow the world will keep spinning and everyone will find a way to move on. This reality must be weaved into the fabric of our ultimate purpose. In determining what our ultimate purpose is we have to consider that we are only here on earth for a limited time, and because of that, our purpose cannot be limited to just our existence.

Understanding why you exist and what you are here to accomplish requires looking outside of yourself. You can't just consider your own agenda, you have to consider something much bigger than 'little old me.'

As a woman of Christian faith, I see my purpose as being wrapped up in God and the things that I believe He wants to accomplish here on earth. I realize that I am only here for a limited lifetime and that God's plan will continue to thrive long after I'm gone. At the end of my life, I want to know that the things I spent my time accomplishing will live on and make a difference. During my time here on earth, I want to be a part of God's plans, I want to make God smile. It's these thoughts that help me to understand the scope of my ultimate purpose.

**Your Gifts**

Gifts are those things that you have a great proficiency in, the things that you're good at (administration, art, fashion, academics, athleticism, etcetera). Instead of thinking about these areas of strength as things you just happen to do well, I encourage you to see them as gifts—things you've been given to help contribute to the world in a special way. We are often conditioned to think about our talents in terms of financial gain and as tools to make our lives better. But instead of just thinking about yourself, I encourage you to consider how your gifts can be used to touch the world and improve the life of someone else.

Your gift has been given to you for a particular time and reason. How would you treat a special present, one that you valued a great deal? You would most likely treasure it and make sure it is treated with care and consideration. Much like a well-loved present from a special person, it is important that we treat our God-given talents with respect and honour.

> Much like a well-loved present from a loved one, it is important that we treat our God-given talents with respect and honour.

Suppose you somehow lost your superior ability or gift, how would you manage to accomplish your ultimate purpose? For example, you sing well and you want to use your talent to entertain the world; but what do you do if you lose your voice? Now what if you said you want to use your voice to worship God? In this case, even if you lose your voice and you are no longer able to sing, you can still worship God.

## Other Purposes and Responsibilities

We don't just have one purpose in life. We may have one ultimate purpose, but we must do more than just that throughout our lifetime. Otherwise, we'll experience much frustration and be a source of frustration to others.

Sometimes we need to do the things we don't necessarily enjoy doing, so that later we can do the things we enjoy. For example, I once worked at a shelter. I had prayed to get that job, but then after I got in, I started praying to get out. While I was there, I begun to realize that it was a step that helped me get to a place where I could use my gift more fully. And even though I wasn't enjoying the process, I had many opportunities while there to fulfill my ultimate purpose.

Your ultimate purpose will inform what you choose to say yes to and what you choose to do with your time and talents. It is imperative to know what your ultimate purpose is because the other two parts of your purpose are connected to this first piece.

**Benefits of Having Purpose**

*Living on purpose*

When you have a clear sense of why you are here, why you've been blessed to wake up this morning, and what you need to accomplish with your life, you will be more deliberate about living your life with intentionality. Instead of just living life aimlessly and allowing your feelings to direct you, you will carefully choose where you invest your time.

Too often people allow their lives and their choices to be dictated by other people's opinions. For some, because your parents and teachers thought you would be a good teacher, you followed their vision for your life and pursued education. For others, because your friends thought it was cooler to hang out at school rather than work hard at getting good grades, you wasted your school years socializing rather than studying.

It's sad how the negative opinions of others influence us. A teacher in high school once told me that I would never get into university, but she was wrong. Dead wrong. I was able to push beyond her opinion of what I could do because I had a clear sense of purpose for my life. I knew that I wanted to be a family therapist and that goal required that I get into university and begin my studies in Psychology. I knew what I needed to do, regardless of that teacher's opinion, because I knew my purpose.

*Increased focus and productivity*

When you know that there is a reason for doing what it is that you do, you will have a sense of excitement that will cause you to focus on getting the job done, not because you *have to* do it, but because you *want to* do it. When you are focused, you can quickly decipher between the things that can wait and the things that need to be done right away. Your productivity will increase when you know what to say *yes* to and what to say *no* to. As a result of your focus, you will end up taking half the time to do what would take another person a full day to accomplish.

*A sense of fulfillment*

Pursuing your purpose allows you to live a life full of meaning. It will give you a constant mindfulness that you have an opportunity and a responsibility to make a difference in the world. And because you recognize that there is an important reason for your life, you will be inclined to act in such a way that your actions will positively affect your community and all those who come across your path.

When you are faced with the challenges that roadblocks bring, you will be empowered to remind yourself that you are working towards something much bigger than your struggle, which will in turn fuel you to push pass your obstacles and pursue your goal relentlessly. At the end of the day when you lay

> Pursuing your purpose allows you to live a life full of meaning.

your head on your pillow, you will experience a sense of fulfilment because of the joy in knowing that you are pursuing exactly what you've been created to do. Even the small steps you make daily will bring you joy because they bring you closer to your goal.

*A final thought*

It's interesting that although God has made us unique and has given each of us a purpose, the world keeps turning after our death. With our last breath, our purpose on earth comes to an end, but the world just keeps on going. This reality helps to affirm my belief that my purpose must be grounded in something bigger than me. My life can't just be about me and my personal goals; there must be more to my existence. While those things are important, I want to be a part of the bigger picture and not get lost in the smaller one.

## Key Questions
### Where Am I Going?

1. What do you understand your purpose to be at this point in your life?
2. What are your strengths and gifts?
3. What would you define as your ultimate purpose?
4. How have you used your gifts to improve the life of someone else?
5. Give an example of how your responsibilities have helped you realize your ultimate purpose?

## Prayer

Dear Lord, you told me, "I know what I'm doing. I have it all planned out—plans to take care of you, not abandon you, plans to give you the future you hope for" (Jeremiah 29:11, MSG). So many of my plans have not materialized yet and I'm beginning to wonder if I really know what I'm doing and where I'm going with my life. I must admit that I don't know the way to achieve my desires on my own. I've tried and failed, and now I'm ready to give you full control. Please show me your heart's desire for my life, and show me how to walk in the way you have destined for me to go.  As I commit to developing a life map, I pray that you will be the compass that points me in the direction I need to go. Help me to grow in confidence as I learn to lean more on you. Help me to find my way. Show me, daily, the path that you have made for me. Walk before me, Lord, and make the pathway straight.

Amen

# Chapter 2
# There Is Only One You

How often do you think about how special it is to be you? Did that question make you laugh? Or did it leave you feeling puzzled? You wouldn't be the first person to minimize how special they are. The truth is we often don't see ourselves as being very special at all.

Give most people an opportunity to talk about their flaws and the things they would love to see improved about themselves and they'd come up with a pretty long list. Ask those same people to list the things they appreciate about themselves and they instantly look like a deer caught in headlights. I have found that people find it hard to talk about their positive qualities because of the way they see themselves.

In today's society, it is easy to feel poorly about ourselves. The message we receive through the media is that we are somehow lacking something and so we are left feeling that we need to buy more or do more in order to measure up. These messages contribute to the stripping away of a person's self-worth and leaves people feeling unhappy with themselves. If a person has any hope of overcoming the continuous berating messages from the world, there needs to be an intentional weeding out of the negative while replacing them with truthful, positive, and empowering thoughts.

You are special. You are unique. You have the capacity for greatness within you. There are things about you that only you possess. Your perception, your experiences, your feelings, and your thoughts are all unique.

It is impossible for any other person to feel, think, or experience life exactly the way you do. There is also no other person alive who can live your life the way you can. The way you walk, talk, express yourself, and do whatever it is that you choose to do will always be unique to you. Even if someone tried to copy you they would fail miserably because there can only ever be one you.

### Failing to Appreciate Your Uniqueness

With all the negativity surrounding us in our North American society it is very easy to see our differences as something undesirable. The truth is no one truly fits into the crowd because the crowd is full of uniquely designed individuals.

I find it amusing when people make drastic efforts to express their individuality. They do something 'attention grabbing' and then when asked to explain what led them to do such a thing, they usually articulate their need to express themselves as distinctive individuals who don't fit into any molds. What makes me smile inside when I hear these types of statements is that just being alive, breathing, and existing, makes you unique, different, and one of a kind. Not because of any drastic efforts you've made, but simply because you were born that way.

Do you realize what is inside of you? When was the last time you sat down and wrote out all the things you like about yourself and the things you have to offer the world? Do you realize the potential you carry? Or do you just focus on comparing yourself to others? When you compare what your assignment is to someone else's, you may begin to believe the lie that what you've been created to do is "not that big of a deal." But when you consider the God who has written your assignment and specifically designed you for that task, you will begin to realize the incredible opportunity you've been given.

The purpose you have may seem similar to that of others you know, however your purpose can only be fulfilled the right way by you. If you are a speaker and you find yourself comparing your style of speaking to someone else's style, you may also find yourself wanting to change your own style. You would be better off just focusing on the message you have to deliver and concentrating on becoming better and better at your delivery style. In a world where people focus so much on fitting in, do yourself a big favour and stop comparing yourself to others. You should only compare yourself to the person you used to be and aim to improve yourself with every speaking opportunity. The Merriam-Webster's dictionary defines the word purpose as "the reason why something is done or used: the aim or intention of something." There is only one you and the reason for which you exist is unlike anyone else's in the entire world. Your ultimate purpose may be similar to many others, but

> There is only one you and the reason for which you exist is unlike anyone else's in the entire world.

the way you go about fulfilling it will be exclusive to you only.

My thoughts on uniqueness:

### 1. There's nothing wrong with saying you're special

People generally stop saying positive things about themselves in adulthood. While children jump at the opportunity to share something about themselves that they are proud of, adults are usually reluctant when it comes to talking about their positive attributes. It is unfortunate that so many of us stop thinking of ourselves as special and lose our sense of pride in the things that make us extraordinary.

We hesitate to celebrate that we are special for fear of not being *special enough*. Comparing ourselves to others will lead us into thinking, "Well, what I have to offer isn't as good as what she has to offer," but the size of our gifts isn't important at all. The important thing is that we recognize that we are all special and uniquely made, and that's something to celebrate.

If you don't make the time to recognize and acknowledge the things about you that are special, who will? Too often we buy into the idea that we must sit around and wait for someone to treat us like we're special, while forgetting that the most important person to recognize our uniqueness is we ourselves. You can't expect others to see what you don't make the time to see yourself.

## 2. Life is more enjoyable when you embrace who you are

Once you've decided to accept yourself, including all your flaws, you will enjoy life a whole lot more. The negative cycle of messages sent to us through mainstream media will never stop; you could do x, y, and z, only to realize that you still don't meet the criteria deemed acceptable.

Once you've decided to accept yourself, you can stop worrying about what others think about you and focus on doing the things that are in your best interest. Life was not only meant to be enjoyed when things are perfectly lined up in the right position, instead you learn how to enjoy life once you admit that there will always be something that needs to be improved and that you are a work in progress. Letting go of the picture perfect image in your mind will allow you to simply enjoy whatever season of life you are currently in.

Accepting yourself is:

- Acknowledging your strengths as well as your areas of growth
- Recognizing that life is a journey that consists of highs and lows
- Being happy being yourself and not trying to be like anyone else
- Being content while working on your flaws

Accepting yourself is not:

- Being self-centred and focusing only on your needs
- Wanting the world to tolerate all your flaws without complaint
- Pretending that you don't have areas that need improvement
- Refusing to improve yourself physically, emotionally, spiritually, and intellectually

3. **No one will ever entirely know and appreciate all of who you are**

A part of appreciating how special you are is also recognizing that you are the only person who will ever come close to understanding everything that makes you who you are. The only other person that knows you more than yourself is God, the One who created you.

We all long to be understood, appreciated, and loved by others, but it's important to realize that while there are people who love and support us, those people cannot be expected to understand all of who we are. I mean think about it, it is hard enough for you to understand yourself, so it would be incredibly difficult for someone else.

Many times we get frustrated and upset with the significant people in our lives because we feel that they should just 'know us,' and know what we want and what we need. But this type of thinking will always leave us feeling disappointed because people around us cannot read our minds, nor do they have a crystal ball to see what our future holds.

So save yourself the frustration and accept that the task of understanding yourself is yours only. As you begin to learn more about yourself, you can then share your insights with the people whom you love in order to help them in understanding you more.

### 4. Accepting yourself makes you more acceptable

Accepting yourself makes you attractive. However, being attractive in this sense doesn't refer to your outer-appearance, but rather to the aura you emit and how people pick up on that. People enjoy being around confident people, people who know who they are and are able to carry themselves with confidence.

> Once you've decided to accept yourself, including all your flaws, you will enjoy life a whole lot more.

As you focus on developing a plan for your life it is important that you are confident that you will accomplish the things you have set out to do. Self-assurance is sometimes used along with the word confidence, and while it is not a bad word, I would encourage you to ask yourself, "What assurance can I have in myself if God isn't leading me?" Self-assurance can only take you so far, but God-assurance can take you all the way!

Growing in the assurance that you will fulfill your purpose in life takes time, but recognizing where your strength comes from will help to minimize that time. While people are attracted to people who are confident, excessive confidence or arrogance becomes overbearing and ends up being a turn off. Therefore, it is important to remain grounded by keeping your focus on the true source of your abilities.

There is only one of you, never has there been and never will there be another you. We've all been "fearfully and wonderfully made" (Psalm 139:14). If even your fingerprint is different from everyone else's, imagine all the other facets of you that are different. Do you appreciate your uniqueness or do you despise it?

At some point as a young girl I began to really despise my voice. I grew up in a musical family where I was always encouraged to sing, so I didn't feel self-conscious about my singing voice. Rather it was my talking voice that made me uncomfortable. I have a very soft voice. I'd never really considered what my voice sounded like until a few boys in my middle school began teasing me about it. I remember one boy in particular, Denton, would repeat everything I said in a soft, high-pitched way, and I would say, "Denton, stop it!" To which he would repeat "De-e-enton, sto-o-op it." And thus, my hatred for my voice began.

From that point forward, I began to take note of people's comments about my voice—both singing and talking. Even if a person didn't mean it as a criticism, I would take their comments as a reminder that my voice sounded different from everyone else's, which I considered something negative. I remember hearing my voice on a tape recorder and cringing at the sound.

It wasn't until my most recent adult years that I began to embrace my voice. And it took God sending me people I would least expect to help me to accept this part of myself. Random people began to point out that they found my voice to be soothing and comforting. Clients would tell me that they appreciated talking with me because my voice was comforting to them. Imagine that. The very thing that the enemy had convinced me to hate as a child became the exact thing that God would use to calm and comfort those in need of encouragement and support. The very thing I wished I could change was the exact tool that God would use to fulfil my purpose. Incredible!

How many things about yourself have you wished were different? How many times have you looked at yourself and said, "If only I could be more like _____ (fill in the blank)." I encourage you to stop allowing the enemy to make you hate parts of yourself. You are not perfect, and that's exactly how God intended you to be.

**There Is Beauty in the Imperfect**

It's so crazy how our culture tries to elevate images and stories of seeming perfection when there is no such thing as perfection. In fact, the people who pretend to be perfect are probably some of the scariest people to be around because they are disconnected from reality. Instead of grieving over our imperfections and beating ourselves up about all that's wrong with us, let us explore what our imperfections can teach us and the beauty it can bring into our lives.

*Humility*

True humility can be found in the person who is aware of just how imperfect they are. A humble woman is able to see herself for who she is—special, but not better than. She recognizes that the same beauty, potential, and promise that is within her also lies within the person standing next to her. Because of that awareness, the person who is truly humble treats others with respect, understanding that her personal thoughts, ideas, opinions, and desires are not more important than anyone else's. Our imperfections give us the humility to see others as we see ourselves.

*Empathy for others*

I find that people tend to confuse the words empathy and sympathy. Sympathy is feeling bad for someone. A sympathetic person might say, "I'm so sorry that happened to you." Empathy, however, takes things one step further by putting oneself in the other person's shoes. Instead of just feeling bad that a person has lost their job, empathy stops, listens, and imagines what it must feel like for that person to experience this loss.

Empathy requires more than just ears, it requires your heart. However, you can't engage in empathy if you are so caught up in how much better you might have dealt with this or that situation. When we recognize our imperfections, we have more empathy for others because we can relate to their flaws and limitations.

*You cling to the perfect One*

Imagine if there was nothing wrong with you, that you woke up every morning on the right side of the bed, had the best outlook for your day, did everything exactly the way you imagined in your mind, and had no struggle reaching the goals you set. Chances are you've never experienced a day like that, neither have I. Unbelievably, though, there are some people who experience many such days, and those people are probably not reading this book because they don't require help fulfilling their goals. I mean, if life goes exactly how you want it to go, without hiccups and roadblocks and imperfections, why would you ever need to look for help? How many times have you had to look up to the heavens and say, "God, this isn't working the way I expected," or "God, I need your help," or "Lord, give me strength"? Christ and the sacrifice He's made for us wouldn't make much sense if we had perfect lives. Therefore, be thankful you have imperfections because it allows you to recognize just how desperately you need the Saviour, the only perfect One, and to Him only should we cling.

*So now what?*

Still struggling to embrace your uniqueness and accept your imperfections? That's okay, welcome to the club, you're not alone. I believe that this task is a continuous work in progress, so don't be discouraged.

One of the best things you can do to help yourself along the journey of self-acceptance is to begin documenting those things about yourself that you consider to be exceptional. Start here:

- List two or three things about yourself that you consider to be unique.
- How can these things help you in fulfilling your purpose?
- Make a list of the things that those closest to you appreciate most about you.

# Key Questions
## There Is Only One You

1. List five things that make you unique

2. How have you embraced your uniqueness?

3. How have you failed to appreciate your uniqueness in the past?

4. How has your uniqueness been used to help someone other than yourself?

# Prayer

Is it true, Lord, that before you shaped me in my mother's womb you knew all about me? That before I saw the light of day you had holy plans for me? (Jeremiah 1:5, MSG) Some days I really have a hard time believing that. You said in Psalm 139:14 that I am fearfully and wonderfully made, but I don't always feel that way. Many days I wonder what is wrong with me, and feel like I have more imperfections than good things about myself to celebrate. Lord, I believe that your word is true, so I am asking that you comfort this insecure heart of mine. Help me to turn to you when I feel overwhelmed by my shortcomings. Teach me to appreciate all that you've created in me.

Show me how you see me and help me to embrace the person you've created me to be.

Amen

# Chapter 3
# Why a Life Map?

What is a life map and why do you need one?

Proverbs 16:9 says, "In their hearts humans plan their course, but the Lord establishes their steps." A life map is a necessity. It is not just something that is helpful, neither is it just a good idea, rather it is a necessary tool that we all need to help us figure out where we are headed.

If you were embarking on a trip to somewhere new, somewhere you had never been before, would you expect to get there without the help of a map or directions? Likewise, it would be foolish for you to wake up one morning, walk out the door, and just start walking aimlessly. If you keep walking you'll end up somewhere, but the chances of you ending up where you want to are slim. We all need a map if we want to successfully arrive at our goal destination.

Ask any successful person to tell you how they ended up where they are today and they will tell you the path they took to get there. Sometimes people who didn't plan to go down a particular path end up on that path and it works out being a great move; but most often when people end up on a path they didn't plan for it leads them in a wrong direction or to a place of frustration and stagnation. Consider the journey you are currently on and contemplate what your next steps will be. Think about your life goals, the vision you have for your future, the things you have control over, and begin to structure a plan for how you will get to your destination.

Committing to a life map is not saying *no* to being flexible, neither is it committing to a rigid, boxed-in life. On the contrary, knowing where you are headed helps you to forecast your route and focus on your journey.

With a life map you can very easily and quickly see when change needs to take place. If you've been sticking to your weekly or monthly goals, and the outcome is unsatisfactory, then you can make adjustments as you see fit. The beauty of having a map is that you get to write the course and have the power to adjust it should it need altering in some way.

Two people may be headed in the same direction. Perhaps their goal sounds similar, like owning their own hair salon for example. The beauty of mapping your own route to your destination is that no two people's maps will look the same. Two people may end up owning their own hair salons, but because each individual is unique and different in so many ways, the things they each have to do to get to 'Opening Day' will result in their day- to-day tasks being different.

Whether people call their path to their destination a life map or not, we all have one. You can either commit yourself to considering your whole life and what you would like to see come out of it, or you could decide to 'fly by the seat of your pants.' It is possible that you could end up seeing some success by simply moving through life

> Your life map considers your dreams and aspirations for your future and helps you set the appropriate goals to get there.

without a plan, but you will undoubtedly get more out of life and your potential by utilizing a life map.

We spend too much time considering, planning, and intending, but never enough time doing. Then when we do end up doing things, they tend not to be the things we considered, planned, and intended to do. Too much of our time gets wasted and in order for this to stop we need to be intentional and committed to making a change towards something more positive; in this case, the creation of a life map. You cannot focus on every aspect of your life at the same time. Likewise, you cannot do a life map that focuses on every area of your life at once. Choose one area that you would like to focus on for a particular time period and focus your energy on accomplishing the goals you've made in that area. Once done, move along to another area of focus, and repeat the process.

A life map is a blueprint of where you want your life to go. It maps out the route to getting to your desired destination in life. Your life map considers your dreams and aspirations for your future and helps you set the appropriate goals to get there. Your life map will consider where you are right now and help you determine what you need to do to move from here to there.

Your life map doesn't consist of the path that someone is encouraging you to take; instead, it focuses on the path that you, by God's leading, desire to take in order to make your dreams your reality. Your life map is a tool that you will use to determine your current and future goals.

What's the difference between the person who is bursting with ambition but does nothing with it and the person who has a goal and gets it done? People who accomplish their goals have the following things in common:

- Vision
- A Plan
- Hope
- Commitment

## 1. Vision

Vision is the ability to see, or the act of anticipating what will or may come to be. When considering your life and your future, what do you see for yourself? What is that thing that you imagine yourself doing? In order to fully answer this question, let's look at the various aspects of your life—professional, personal, spiritual, and physical—individually.

What areas of your life do you feel the need to focus on? It is impossible to work on every aspect of your life simultaneously, so be sure to focus on one area at a time. For each aspect of your life, ask yourself, "What is missing in this area at the moment?" and "What do you envision changing in this area?" Write it down. How will your life improve once this vision becomes reality? Write that down, too.

Now give this vision a name. For example, if the vision for your professional life is to practice law, then name the vision *"My life as a lawyer."* Know that there is much power in writing down and declaring your vision (see Habakkuk 2:2). You can even go further by writing a mission statement. As life progresses, you will understand more of what it is that you want for your life. As you allow God to direct you, He will also show you the different areas in which He desires to use you.

I've always known that I love to talk; in fact, all my report cards in middle school and high school would highlight that fact. As I've grown, I've seen how my talkative and open nature has led to people being drawn to confide in me. Therefore, going to school to learn how to be a great counsellor and therapist was a no-brainer. But learning that I have the gift of encouragement was something that

I grew into and that God slowly revealed to me. I knew that I wanted to see people achieve the positive change they were longing for, which seemed natural for a therapist. But discovering that I was passionate about seeing God's truth fulfilled in the lives of the people I came into contact with took some time.

I used to always wonder why I was so irritated by certain preachers that I would listen to. It took me a very long time to accept that the reason I was frustrated was because I was also called to preach and teach the word of God, which made me desire for it to be done well. I was also called to lead and challenge people to action. I was called to move people beyond the excitement they experience after a great sermon to the place where they actually do something life-changing with the word they've received. It took me a long time to identify and accept those things about myself.

## 2.  A Plan

Once you have written out your vision, the next step is to devise a plan to accomplish it. Ask yourself the following questions:

- What do I need to do to accomplish this goal?
- How did other people doing what I envision doing achieve success?
- How long will it take me?
- What will it cost me?
- Who can help me?
- What are the steps involved?
- What will my first step be?

Sometimes people get stuck at this point because they worry about not knowing all the steps it will take to make their dreams a reality. What's important is that you start with the first step that comes to mind and slowly proceed from there.

Other people spend so much time coming up with the plan and trying to make it perfect that they end up wasting away precious 'action' time, and end up delaying getting anything done

## 3. Hope

It is easy to become excited about the potential of seeing your vision accomplished. However, sooner or later, reality sets in—actualizing your dream takes time and this can sometimes be frustrating. We live in the microwave age where we want things completed instantly, without having to wait. Unfortunately, pursuing your vision will take some time, and so it is important not to lose hope on your journey to accomplishing what you've seen.

This is *your* vision, so you need to stay encouraged and motivated. It is natural to begin to question whether your goal is truly worth working for, and it is natural to begin to lose faith in yourself, but you must not give up hope. Instead, surround yourself with encouragers who will remind you that you can accomplish what you've set out to do. You need to maintain the hope that what you are doing is going to make a difference in the world around you. You must continue to grow your faith and tap into those things that motivate you to keep pressing.

**Commitment**

There is a big difference between having the desire to do something and having the commitment to actually get that thing done. Having passion for something is important as it will give you a great start, but it cannot sustain you. In order to fulfill your goal you will need to be intentional and consistent. Starting and stopping leads to failure. It's pointless to start working out and eating well, then going back to your old, unhealthy ways, because it only undoes what you've spent all that time doing to be healthy.

Businesses have vision and mission statements because it is important for every employee to know what that business is striving towards. Policies and procedures, rules and regulations are all set in place with the intention of ensuring that the vision and mission are accomplished. We, too, need to know what our

> Pursuing your vision will take some time, and so it is important not to lose hope on your journey to accomplishing what you've seen.

personal mission is and our rules of engagement in ensuring that we accomplish our vision and mission. A clear vision and mission statement indicates where a company is going. Likewise, a clear life map will determine where you are going and keep you on track with your final outcome.

Are you hesitant about writing a mission statement? Think of your life as being no less important than a successful and thriving business. If successful business owners see the importance of planning ahead to ensure their success, why should your life be any different? Your life is just as important as any thriving enterprise. Recognize that you're bursting with potential, and once you do you can approach your pursuits with the same kind of commitment a CEO has for the business she is running.

Coming up with a mission statement can be helpful as you embark on developing your life map. There are many different ways to develop a mission statement. Start by writing out:

- What you want to accomplish with your life at the end of the day (e.g. to help people, to be joyful, to be grateful)
- What means/tools you can use to achieve that mission (e.g. help others through my skills as a counsellor)
- What this will accomplish in your community and the world at large (e.g. help make my community a happier place to be)

Once you've figured out those three things, combine them into one statement. For example, *"I want to be fulfilled by helping others with my skills as a counsellor in order to make my community a happier place to be."*

Once you have figured out your personal mission, you're now ready to start working on your life map with commitment and passion.

## What Does a Life Map Include?

1. List of your strengths and areas for growth
2. List your dreams, ambitions, and goals
3. List of your areas of focus
4. A timeline
5. List of people and resources for support
6. List of potential roadblocks
7. Plans for staying motivated
8. Running sheet of other goals to be pursued in the future

## Key Questions
Why a Life Map?

1. Why do you need a life map?

2. What is a dream or goal that you've been carrying in your heart?

3. How will your life improve by accomplishing this goal?

4. What will your first step be towards achieving this goal?

## Prayer

Beginning something new is both daunting and exciting at the same time. Holy Spirit, be my comfort during this time of adjustment. I desire to see my life in a new light. I want to be more aware of the steps I need to take. I want to consider the destiny you have for me as I walk along this journey. Just 'going with the flow' hasn't allowed me to fulfill your purpose for my life; so Lord, I'm asking you to help me as I embark on this new way of living. When my old habits want to take over and bring me off course, give me the strength to stand strong and follow through with the map you've given me.

Amen

# Chapter 4
## Step 1: Make a Choice and Make it Matter

Knowing where to start is by far one of the hardest things to nail down when considering life goals and ambitions. We have all been created with an enormous amount of potential and it's sad to think about how much potential is left untapped by so many in this world. Hence, it's never a matter of *if* a person has the potential to do great things, but more so a question of *which* great thing a person should pursue at a given point in time.

Given the fact that you likely have more than one goal for your life, when writing your map be very clear about what goal you will be focusing on during a specific period of time. We've been created as multi-talented and multi-gifted beings that have many responsibilities, passions, and dreams. It is therefore very easy to become overwhelmed with the many things that we would like to accomplish. It can also be very difficult to figure out which areas to focus on first. Don't make the mistake, however, of trying to focus on every idea that comes to mind, for this will eventually lead to burn out and the inability to do anything well.

It is necessary to narrow down your focus if you are going to be successful at reaching your goals in life. I remember the challenges I experienced in my early adulthood as I tried to figure out exactly what to pursue. From time to time, I still find it hard to narrow my focus when new ideas come to my mind.

For as long as I can remember, I've always been very passionate about three things: helping people, music, and drama. When it came time to decide what to focus on in my post-secondary studies, I struggled with which area to pursue. I decided to pursue the area of helping people, and so I studied Psychology and later did my graduate studies in Marriage and Family Therapy.

I don't regret pursuing the area of interest that I chose. However, I do often wonder how much stronger I would've been in the areas of music or drama had I committed as much time and dedication to them as I did to counselling. I'm sure that many of you can relate when you consider which avenue you decided to go down in life, but hopefully you don't have regret.

The good news is that regardless of how you feel about your past choices, as long as you are living and breathing, you still have the opportunity to choose a different path to explore. God has blessed us with many choices in life that fall within the path He has set out for us to travel. He may be encouraging you to be an artist or to open up a small business, but within that one area there are so many different avenues, styles, and ways in which you can fulfill that call.

Sometimes it's hard to hear the voice of God and know without a shadow of a doubt that one particular way of pursuing something is the right way to go. In fact, it can be quite confusing and discouraging at times. As a result, we often get caught up waiting on God to show us exactly what every step on the path should look like. The Bible says that God is the Shepherd who speaks and we are His sheep who hear His voice. Therefore, be assured that God is speaking to you, even as you read these pages. God speaks to you through the Bible, through creation, and through people. He uses ways we sometimes don't even consider to speak to our hearts, so don't ever stop seeking to hear His voice.

I believe that the journey of self-discovery is something that is done with the help of the Lord, and is a life-long journey. The process cannot be rushed, so any attempt to speed it up will be futile. You know what you know about yourself because God decided to reveal it to you. The same can be said about your path in life. God will reveal to you only what He chooses to let you know at any given time.

> Regardless of how you feel about your past choices, as long as you are living and breathing, you still have the opportunity to choose a different path to explore.

My mission in writing *The Life Map* is to help you become more mindful of the fact that God has a plan for your life, which He is revealing to you daily. Making your map will help to ensure that you are ready and able to hear where it is that He is leading and directing you.

There is something that God has impressed on your heart to accomplish with your gifts and talents. Do you know what that is? Have you taken the time to seek God's direction concerning your life and what He wants it to look like? This book will guide you in writing out the map as you sense God leading you.

We all have different areas of focus for different seasons in life. For example, in high school, your goal might have been to get into a particular post-secondary institution. In university, your goal might have been to earn a certain grade point average to get on to the honour roll and qualify for graduate studies. As you age, your goals will expand and evolve according to the season you are in.

The beauty of your life map is that you will do it over and over again throughout your life for different areas and seasons. It will provide a framework for you to plan out how you will fulfil your various ambitions in life. It will also help you consider areas of your life that you may not have been considering in terms of goal setting. Life is a journey, and on that journey there are many paths that you can choose to travel. Sometimes we find ourselves wondering "What if I travelled down that other path?" Even worse, we get stuck at a cross point.

The big picture can at times be overwhelming, and we can forego starting anything because the vision seems intimidating and unattainable. But you mustn't allow the bigness of your dreams to stop you from achieving them. The key to accomplishing a big goal is to find a way to break the big picture down into smaller goals, and then make the first step. Case in point, if you want to start a wedding décor business, there are many different ways to go about pursuing this goal. For some people, they might start by getting business cards, a website, and offer their services for free or at a very low rate to gain experience and clientele. Other individuals might begin by taking a small business course, volunteering with another wedding décor company to learn how to operate a small business, and then they might create a business plan with a six-month plan to launch out on their own.

Depending on your style, experience, and God's leading, you can begin to write down the possible steps you could take to achieve your goal, and then narrow those steps down to the steps you will choose to follow. It isn't necessary to say that this is the only way to pursue a particular dream because research will show that others have achieved a goal like yours using a variety of different ways.

I believe that most of the things people dream about are possible. Unfortunately, though, many folks don't end up realizing their dreams because of self-doubt, discouragement, past hurts, or simply because they didn't have the map to make it happen.

What do you do when you are not 100% sure about what you should be doing? I went out with a friend one day and she asked me, "Colleen, how did you know that working with women, doing conferences, workshops, and Bible studies was what you were meant to do? What solidified things for you and helped you see that this avenue was exactly where you needed to go?" I absolutely loved that question, even though I'd never really considered it before. I did my best to answer from my heart and I thought to myself, "I need to really commit myself to thinking more about this and writing it down."

When I consider where I am in my life, professionally— author, therapist, and speaker—I know I am exactly where I am supposed to be. As I look back over my life, I can see how all the pieces have worked together to create what I'm now living out as my life. From a spiritual perspective, I can see very clearly how God has orchestrated my life's experiences to shape and mould me into the woman I have become. I can see how the things I experienced in childhood trained and prepared me for exactly what I'm doing now.

I believe that I've been able to confidently state what I'm called to do because I've done my best to always say *yes* to God when I feel Him leading me. When I felt the call to be a therapist, I did what made sense to do—I applied for various programs.

I had my preferences, but I didn't let my preferences supersede my *yes*. So if I wanted to go to university X but university Y was the one that accepted me, then that's where I went. I also said *yes* to God when He put the idea of the conference on my heart. I said *yes* when He put the spoken word devotional *A Call to Worship* on my heart. I then said *yes* when He encouraged me to give the keynote speech at my conference. With every *yes* and every task, I became more confident. Then came the Bible study, then the workshop series, and then the call to write this book emerged as an urgent 'must' on my list.

## Things to Consider When Choosing the First Step:

- Is it in your control?

- Are you passionate about it?

- Is it SMART (specific, measurable, achievable, realistic, time-bound)?

*Is it in Your Control?*

While I agree with dreaming big and reaching for the stars, we need to be honest with ourselves enough to admit that there are things that are out of our control. I had a friend who once told me that her goal for the next five years was to get married, go back to school, and start a family. I thought to myself, "Hmm, why would she set a goal like that when she only had control over one of those three things?" I didn't share my thoughts with her at the time, but I left that conversation feeling concerned that my friend had put herself in a situation where she had no

> There is a need to differentiate between the things that you have some control over versus the things that you have no control over.

control over the goals she had set. I knew she would ultimately feel bad if those goals weren't met when truthfully they were not in her control to begin with.

What can you do to ensure that the goals that are out of your control (like meeting an ideal mate and getting married) are fulfilled? You could work on improving your confidence, improving the outlook you have on your life and towards yourself, and making yourself as attractive as you possibly can. And while those choices might make you a more attractive person, they cannot guarantee that you will find the man or woman of your dreams and get married.

There is a need to differentiate between the things that you have some control over versus the things you have no control over. You could work your behind off and get the highest marks in your field of study, yet still there is no guarantee that you will get the dream job you are waiting on. Yes, there are things we can all do to improve the likelihood that certain things will happen for us, but there is no way to guarantee how the other factors involved will work out.

*Are you passionate about it?*

Do you feel excited when you think about your goal? It is essential for you to be passionate about your ambitions, for without passion life is bland and colourless. Some people hesitate to strive for passion and end up settling for mediocrity because they convince themselves that striving for passion is being overly dramatic. Yet while those of us who are more dramatic might find it easier to connect with passion, it is important not to confuse the two. Passion is something that is felt; it wells up from deep within and pushes you towards what is important. Passion gives you the push and drive to relentlessly pursue your ambitions.

I feel strongly about the things that are important to me—God, my family, my friends, the things I do with my time and energy. And not only am I a very sensing person, I am also a very expressive person. That's just the way God made me. People often think of passion as being associated with romance, but regardless of your relationship status, passion is something that is important to have, whether we are involved in a romantic relationship or not.

Passion is one of the gifts we have that makes life interesting, exciting, and memorable. I was once addicted to romance novels. I would finish one book and scramble to find a new book quickly. I was addicted to how reading and getting lost in the books made me feel.

I remember thinking to myself, "I never knew I would be so happy sitting down by myself with a book." But it wasn't the joy of reading that I'd found, but rather the joy of *feeling* that those particular books stirred within me. I would wake up excited to pick up my book, and I would hurry through the tasks of my day just so I could settle in my corner and read.

The push to keep turning the page and to keep reading comes to mind whenever I think about passion. It's the thing that pushes us to keep going, to keep giving, and to keep pushing. Passion is the desire to not stop, even when it's past the hour for you to go to bed, even when you know you're going to show up to work the next day with bloodshot eyes. Passion is not just a strong feeling of enthusiasm or excitement for something. In some ways, passion is life itself, it's like the life-giving air we breathe.

How have you typically defined passion? Does it play a significant role in the things you dedicate your time to? Oftentimes we find ourselves committed to many things we aren't passionate about. We all have responsibilities in life that may or may not incite passion within us, but beyond those responsibilities, we should strive to spend our personal time on things that give us the wings to fly.

It is easy to have a full life and not feel like you have time for anything else, including the things you are passionate about. It's also very possible to float through life without feeling passionate about anything. A passionless life is a painful life because it was never the way God created us to live. John 10:10 tells us that "the thief comes only to steal, kill and destroy; I have come that they may have life, and have it to the full." A full life is a life that includes all the blessings that God has promised. A full and abundant life is one that is full of passion and purpose.

Purpose and passion aren't the only pieces necessary to make life successful, but they are a great place to start. They make up the foundation of all the things we do with our time and energy.

*Is it SMART?*

The November 1981 issue of Management Review featured an article by George T. Doran called "There's a S.M.A.R.T. way to write management's goals and objectives." It discussed the importance of objectives and the difficulty of setting them. Since then, people have used SMART Goals to represent various terms, the most popular of which is:

S – Specific

The goal must be crystal clear and as detailed as possible so as to ensure that it is easily understood by anyone who hears it. For example, a person might state the following as his goal: "I want to get healthy." In order to make that goal more specific, a person might say, "I want to get physically healthy by changing my diet, increasing my activity level, and losing weight." The second description clears up any confusion someone might have about the details of the goal.

M – Measurable

How can the goal be measured? There must be a way to gauge when the goal has been achieved. For example, in regards to the above goal, the goal-setter would state that not only does he want to increase his physical health, but he also wants to lose twenty pounds by going to the gym five days a week and cutting out all forms of sugar from his diet. That way the goal can be measured by reviewing his week, his sugar intake, and his weight for pounds lost or gained.

A – Achievable

What will it cost you financially, emotionally, time-wise to accomplish your goal? A goal needs to be something you can confidently achieve. This requires knowing your strengths as well as your areas of growth. It makes no sense to set a goal that you don't have the capacity to accomplish.

R – Realistic

Some goals are achievable, yet unrealistic for the goal-setter due to the time they were set or other surrounding circumstances. A person should therefore be honest with himself and decide whether the goal is realistic at the present time. The question therefore is not just 'Can this be done?' but also 'Should this be done?' If your goal isn't realistic for your life at this time, then trying to accomplish it may set you back instead of bring you closer to your ultimate goal.

T – Time-based

Goals must have a deadline. Without deadlines we tend to let our goals linger, and sometimes they never get accomplished at all. Instead of saying, "I want to start working on my website next month," give a specific date. Then set another goal for when you want your website to go live. When these dates are connected to your goal, they serve as motivation for you to do the work required to accomplish the goal.

**How to Increase Your Passion**

*Keep a clear view of your purpose*

Grapple with the *whys*—Why am I interested in this goal? Why is this endeavour so important for me to pursue? How will my life be positively influenced by going after this goal? What will happen if I do not pursue this goal?

Understanding that God has put something inside of you to fulfill, and is pushing you to complete that thing, also consider what God thinks about your goal.

*Give yourself permission to feel*

Having the ability to feel and express our emotions is a blessing from God. We've been created with the capacity to feel many different emotions, and so giving ourselves permission to feel them is a great way to keep passion alive within us. You must become more aware of how you're doing on an emotional level and ask yourself the question, "What am I feeling?" regularly. As you do so, you will become more familiar with the array of emotions that exist within you.

> We've been created with the capacity to feel so many different emotions, and giving ourselves permission to feel them is a great way to keep passion alive within us.

There are things that you will be passionate about that won't move others around you to feel a thing. That is because you have a unique purpose that has been creatively inscribed on your heart. As God reveals more

69

and more of the person He's created you to be, you will increasingly identify the things that stir up your passion.

Be open to experiencing passion; don't be afraid of it or too hesitant to express it. Rather develop a posture that allows you to receive the passion you want. If you are closed off, hesitant, and too concerned about how to act 'just right,' you will miss passion when it presents itself and just end up staying in the cold, mundane safety of an average life.

*Surround yourself with passionate people*

There's nothing more exhausting than hanging out with people who are negative and toxic. Those who lack passion in their lives are equally exhausting. Whenever you share your heart or your dreams with them, they somehow suck the life right out of you.

On the other hand, when you spend time with passionate people their passion comes out of them and bounces onto you. They have a way of making you see just how exciting life can be. Their passion is contagious and that's exactly why you need to be around these people whenever you desire to increase the passion in your life.

*Ask for it*

Psalm 84:11 says that our heavenly Father is a sun and shield. He gives grace and glory, and no good thing will He withhold from them that walk uprightly. That means if you are lacking passion, you can ask God and He will show you exactly how to receive it.

*How can passion help us?*

As mentioned earlier, passion gives us drive, motivation, and that extra push that we need every now and then. It is the gas that keeps the engine going. Passion helps make life enjoyable and allows us to press on even when things don't go our way. When other people say maybe this is a good time to stop, passion encourages you to keep on pressing.

*How can passion get in our way?*

While it is necessary to have passion as you pursue your goals, passion, like your heart, needs to be guarded. Unbridled passion can lead us off course. We have been created with emotions for a reason, but emotions should not take over our decision making functions. Going solely with our emotions can get us into a lot of trouble

# Key Questions
## Step 1: Make a Choice and Make it Matter

1. What are some of your gifts?

2. How can you walk out your gifts in your day-to-day life?

3. What are some of the ideas that you have in your heart to pursue?

4. What makes the most sense to begin pursuing right now?

5. What are the things that you would like to pursue but have no control over?

6. What does passion mean to you?

# Prayer

Some days I don't even know where to start, Lord. I know there is much potential inside of me, and I know that there are many ways in which I can spend my time. The question is: which venture should I pursue at this present time? I am afraid of making mistakes and slowing down the progress in my life. I don't want to experience more wasted time, so I need to know which way to go. I have tried going with my gut in the past but I ended up in a terrible place. Dear Holy Spirit, I need you now. Will you please help me decide my next move?  I pray for your peace to fill me as a sign that you are with me.

Amen

# Chapter 5
# Step 2: Write the Vision and Make it Plain

### The Ambitious Busy Body

There was once a young woman who was very ambitious. She had a natural knack for getting stuff done, and amongst her peers she was seen as someone who always did things with excellence. If she was putting on an event, it was done well. If she was asked to participate in something, she was there on time, with bells on, and did it well. She developed a reputation for being reliable and very capable. For that reason, people always reached out to her for help when they wanted to get something done well. There was only one small problem with this young woman. Although she was very talented and had a great track record for getting things done, she had even bigger dreams in her heart that she wanted to accomplish.

Deep down she knew she had what it took to make this dream a reality, and year after year she would talk about getting it done "this year." But around September or October of each year, the sad reality would hit that this dream was just not going to get done, again. Finally, this young woman hit a point in her life where she broke.

It might have been turning thirty-five and realizing that she was five years away from forty, maybe it was her baby starting his first day of school, or maybe it was realizing that the last pair of jeans that once fit comfortably was now too tight. Whatever it was, she finally reached her breaking point and allowed herself to admit that she was fed up and needed to make a change.

She was fed up with feeling disappointed, year after year, and keeping all the promises she made to others while not keeping the promises she made to herself. Something had to give, but she didn't know what. She determined in her heart that she wouldn't just continue life as usual. She took a leap of faith and talked to a trusted friend who referred her to a life coach. With the help of her coach, she was able to narrow things down. She scored high in the areas of ambition, passion, and desire, but in the areas of planning and following through she scored low. These were the areas in her life where she needed to grow.

With further analysis she discovered that while she had envisioned completing her goal, she had never taken the time to write it out. She'd never written out exactly what she wanted to accomplish in detail, and she hadn't taken the time to consider the steps she would have to take in order to see this goal realized.

So right there in her coach's office she took a sheet of lined paper, grabbed a pen, and began to write. She brought it home and the next day she wrote some more. The next month she wrote even more. And she continued to write until it was accomplished.

While this 'young woman' is a fictional character, we can all relate to many of the feelings and thoughts of what this fictional character was experiencing. I wonder which areas you felt you could relate to most of her story?

**What's the Plan?**

Can you imagine a group of contractors showing up to the construction site and not having a blueprint for what they are working on? How much work do you think would be accomplished? While they have the tools, the skills, and the know-how to build many things, they would not be able to accomplish anything until someone showed up with the blueprint for the job they needed to complete that day.

Your life is no different. You wake up daily with the resources and skills to accomplish great things; however, without having a blueprint for what you will do with the hours you've been given, you won't accomplish much. And should you actually accomplish a lot, it's very unlikely that what you accomplish will fit into the vision you have for your life. It's been said that failing to plan is planning to fail. I have come to realize the truth of this statement, and I hate the feeling I get whenever I miss out on the opportunity to plan ahead and end up paying for my lack of preparation. Sometimes, it's failing to organize my schedule in a way that allows me to have the time I need to prepare for a speaking engagement. Other times, it is as simple as not taking the time to organize what the children are wearing the next day. Whatever the scenario, I always know that I've missed the opportunity to plan because the next day I am usually scrambling like a chicken without its head. I'm left either running late or missing out on the opportunity to do something of leisure that I would have appreciated doing but no longer have the time for because I have to catch up on what I left undone. These examples may seem trivial, but it is interesting how these seemingly unimportant things can impact what you end up accomplishing with your day.

The vision for your life can be seen in the same way. You may want to go back to school one day, or open a business, or take your health more seriously, but if you fail to put a plan in place for accomplishing that goal, I can promise you that it won't happen, it just won't.

Writing out the vision for your life is a necessary step in accomplishing the goals you have for your life. This step is exciting because you are giving yourself the permission to dream. You will finally be able to do something tangible with all those great ideas that fill your mind as you lay in bed, those dreams you hesitate to share with others for fear that they might look at you like you have two heads.

> Writing out the vision for your life is a necessary step in accomplishing the goals you have for your life.

Writing the vision is the first step in the planning process. When you sign up for a program at school, you know what the end result will be—a degree, certificate, or diploma in a particular subject. At the beginning of the course you are given the schedule for what is required of you throughout the year. If you choose to complete the assignments and do them well, you will receive the degree, certificate, or diploma. However, if you fail to complete the tasks assigned, you will not be given anything. The vision for the program is written out at the beginning of the course, and your job is to meet the requirements of each assignment if you want to make the vision your reality.

In the Old Testament, the prophet Habakkuk was instructed to write the vision and make it plain so that the people would see what they were striving for. Without vision you will not know where you are going in your life, whether financially, professionally, spiritually, or personally. Proverbs 29:18 tells us that where there is no vision the people perish, throw off restraint, and are lawless. Most people are filled with ideas, but not everyone will realize their dreams in life. Activating a plan is key to realizing your dreams. However, you cannot activate a plan if you aren't willing to write it down.

I grew up in a small church in Ottawa, Ontario, and every year during our New Year's Eve service the pastor, who happened to be my dad, would invite everyone to begin the year by writing God a letter. The letter was an opportunity to talk to the Lord about our hopes and what we would like the coming year to look like. Once completed, we would each seal our letters in our own individual envelope with our name on it and then place it in the church's prayer box. The letters would be prayed over throughout the year and at the following New Year's Eve service we would get the letters back so we could be reminded of where we were the year before.

Opening and re-reading the letters written the year before was an opportunity to reflect on all the requests that God had been faithful to grant, as well as a reminder of the requests that we still needed to pray for in the following year. Re-reading the letters also demonstrated how some of the issues that seemed so pressing 365 days earlier were no longer as pressing and were now less of a concern.

I loved writing that yearly letter as a young girl and I love that we still continue that tradition today. In fact, I don't wait till the service to write out my New Year's Eve letter anymore. I begin praying about the letter early in December and I ask God to show me what I need to focus on for the coming year. Over the years, I have come to realize that if I didn't have the opportunity to write down the things that were pressing on my heart and bring them to God, then I might have missed out on the opportunity to reflect on God's faithfulness to listen then, and His faithfulness to listen now.

**Where to Start**

As you prepare to write out your vision, I recommend getting a journal or some type of notebook so you can keep your ideas together in one place. There are times when you will have to jot ideas down on scrap paper or even on a napkin at the restaurant, either way be sure to take that piece of paper and put it in your notebook.

*Writing out the vision*

What is the dream that you carry on the inside? Don't hold back, give yourself permission to write out the things that keep you up at night, the ideas that bombard your mind and consume your thoughts. While you may have some unrealistic dreams, it is important that you allow yourself a space to express what is inside of you. For example, you may close your eyes and dream of being the next pop star to break all the record charts. While there is no exact formula to ensure that being the next big pop star will be your reality, you can begin to map out a platform that you can use to share your musical talent with the world.

*Does it have a name?*

Sometimes what we long to accomplish is clear and it has a name that is easily identifiable, such as becoming a nurse, starting a trucking company, and so on. However, some goals are less clear and require time for a name to develop. For example, a friend of mine named Natasha has always been very creative and took pride in doing an outstanding job at whatever she did. She was especially known for giving great gifts. It wasn't that her gifts were extravagant or expensive; instead, what made her gifts special was that she took extra care in how she picked out and packaged each one. So much so, her recipients always felt special when they received her gifts.

Natasha would hear, time and time again, just how much folks enjoyed receiving gifts from her and attending the parties she threw. Then her friends began asking her to put together gifts for their friends and family members. Eventually, her pastor's wife, my mom, encouraged her to make a business out of this gifting ability. As Natasha prayed and thought about this idea, she struggled with naming exactly what it was that she did. When she sat down and considered all that she had to offer in her business, it was a lot more than just packaging great gifts. She also planned parties, sat on committees that organized conferences, was a personal shopper, did swag bags, and so much more. It took her a while to hammer down what services she offered. Eventually, she came up with the idea of being a one-stop-shop for all things events, a concierge service that would make people's events a success.

Like Natasha, there are many who struggle to sort out exactly what they have to offer. Take the necessary time to think and prayerfully consider how God is leading you in the area of your vision. In time, He will help you name the vision He has given you.

*What need does it fulfil in your community and the world at large?*

When you close your eyes and think about the people around you, how does this vision benefit them? How will this vision make a positive impact on the world? If your vision is primarily self-focused, it won't keep you satisfied for very long. However, when you focus on others you will be repeatedly fulfilled whenever you see the way in which your contribution positively impacts their lives.

Don't get sidetracked with wanting your vision to make a huge wave in the ocean. Focus on making your contribution an excellent one, and let God decide how big that ripple will be. Too often we take our focus off of impacting others and focus instead on how we will look to others. We ask ourselves, "Will my community think this is a great project/idea/business?" Whenever we focus on the opinions of others rather than on giving of ourselves, we miss the mark.

*How does it fulfill you and bring you satisfaction?*

Operating in your purpose will always give you a sense of fulfillment because you are doing what you were created to do. There is a particular kind of joy that comes from operating in your calling and getting a clear sense that God is smiling on your work. In the movie *Chariots of Fire,*

Eric Liddell's character says, "I believe God made me for a purpose, but He also made me fast. And when I run I feel His pleasure." So it is with each of us, when we find ourselves doing what we've been created to do, we can liken it to being in 'the zone'—you feel it, others see it, and I believe that as God watches from on high He is greatly pleased.

*How does it accomplish God's purpose for your life?*

What do you sense that God wants to accomplish through your life? How will it be accomplished through the venture you are embarking on? Never make the mistake of making your plans first, then checking in with God last. Consider the above questions at the onset of your life map and allow the Lord to help

> Be careful not to allow your desires to override God's desires for your life.

you answer them. He will show you if your motives and ambitions are not in alignment with where He is leading you. Be careful also not to allow your desires to override God's desires for your life. Oftentimes, we become focused on making something of our lives or doing something with our lives to make us feel good. Unfortunately, feelings are fleeting and can't always be trusted, so it's better to keep your eyes focused on the things of God. He never changes and we can always trust His will for our lives.

*Where is God leading you?*

You can't write your story alone because you are not the author of your story, God is. Writing the vision for your life, therefore, must be done with the help of the Lord. God's will and purpose is the only thing that will prevail in the end, so before you get started you need to identify where He is leading you.

My husband and I, like many other couples, have had difficult decisions to make regarding life and family. During a challenging time when I was waiting on God to show me what to do in a particular situation, we were encouraged by one of my mentors, Pastor Doug Schneider, to consider how we think God might be leading us. Sometimes we hesitate in our decisions because we haven't heard clearly what God is saying, or we resist making a definitive decision for fear of having heard wrong. There are many difficult decisions that one has to make in life, and when you consider how these decisions can impact you and those around you it makes sense that you prayerfully consider the steps you take.

Nonetheless, in the midst of waiting on God, it is important not to end up doing nothing out of the fear of making a mistake. In the example above, we were forced to dig a little deeper when asked to consider what we thought God was saying. Everyone has thoughts, opinions, and gut feelings, so give yourself permission to say, "Lord, this is what I think, sense, or feel you are saying." If you sense that God is saying nothing, then continue doing the last thing you heard Him say to you.

Don't allow the enemy to hang your fears of walking outside of the will of God over your head, because God will alert you when you step out of His will. It could be through doors being closed, a lack of peace in your spirit, or simply realizing that what you are doing doesn't line up with His word. Regardless of the method He chooses, God will always get through to you and you will know when you are walking out of sync with Him.

*Unanswered questions*

I believe that God uses unanswered questions as a way of getting our attention. As God leads you on the path to your purpose, He will reveal to you questions that need to be answered. Your job isn't to have all the answers, and don't expect that He will reveal all the answers to you immediately. For now, just write down the questions. Note the ones to which you believe He has given you an answer. For the others, simply indicate that you are unsure. Prayerfully revisit those questions and trust that God will reveal the answers you need in His time.

I believe in the importance of good questions, questions that demand answers throughout the course of your life. Regardless of how you come across these questions—the voice of God, a book, a counsellor, a teacher, a pastor, or a close friend—they should be given your attention and deserve answers. Writing these questions down allows you to keep track of them and the answers you receive.

*Failures*

Do yourself a favour. Don't skip this section! I know it's hard to think about the things you've failed at in your life, but the truth is, we can learn so much from our failures.

First, be reminded that everyone has failed or is failing at something in their lives, so you aren't alone.

What are some of the things that you have tried to accomplish in your life that didn't pan out? How long ago did these things happen? How did you respond to your unmet goal? Were you able to press pass the disappointment and find another way to make it happen for you? Have you given up on pursuing that goal or is it still lingering inside of you, waiting to be fulfilled?

It's important to understand how you work, which includes how you deal with failure. Failure has the potential to devastate a person's life, but it doesn't have to be that way. Failure can help us figure out the best way to use our strengths and teach us how to navigate around our areas of weakness. I once had a friend who only shared about the things that were going well for her in her life. She never let down her guard to talk about the issues she was struggling with, and I don't recall ever hearing her admit to failing at anything in her life. Ultimately, our friendship came to a close because I realized that the type of relationship we had was one-sided. Being a very transparent person, I found myself sharing my ups and downs, my struggles and my triumphs, but it wasn't being reciprocated. I eventually realized that I couldn't be a part of her game.

I've concluded that she either didn't know how or perhaps she didn't see me as a safe person to share her failures with, but regardless of the reason, choosing not to acknowledge your failures will only hold you back in life. It negatively affects the relationships you're in because people will either feel that you're not being truthful or they won't feel like they can relate to you. Furthermore, you won't get to a place where you can truly appreciate Christ's ability to walk with you and show you the way out. Therefore, be honest with yourself and with God about your failures.

# Key Questions
## Step 2: Write the Vision and Make it Plain

1. Does your vision have a name?

2. What do you *think* God is saying to you right now about your goal?

3. What have you ever tried to accomplish but failed?

4. Are you honest about your failures?

# Prayer

Lord, I'm tired of falling off course and ending up confused and discouraged. I am praying for your leading as I write the vision for my goal. I admit that I don't have the wisdom to do it on my own; without your hand leading me, I am lost. I commit my plans to you and ask that you use them for your glory. May my efforts be used to fulfill your purpose here on Earth.

Amen

# Chapter 6
## Step 3: Supporting Cast

We cannot make it on our own; hence the saying, "no man is an island." We've been created to live with others, so when it comes to walking out our life map, we cannot do it alone. It may seem safer to think, "The only person I need is me," but even when you are giving 100% you'll still need the support and resources of others to bring your vision to pass.

John Maxwell once said, "Teamwork makes the dream work!" I started repeating the phrase in my conversations and found that other people would nod their heads and finish the statement for me. I was surprised that it wasn't an entirely new concept, and I felt disappointed that it had taken me so long to learn of its existence. Regardless of how long it takes for us to be introduced to helpful concepts, the most important thing is for us to apply these truths whenever we discover them. So, who are the people and what are the resources that you will need to get to your destination?

Who's on your team? The thought of building and leading a team might be intimidating to you. It can also seem quite scary to open up your heart and share something that is near and dear to you with the world. We tend to worry if what we have set out to do will be accepted by those around us, but including others is a necessary step.

A team doesn't have to be a large group of people who are intimately involved with each and every aspect of your goal. Depending on what you are pursuing, your team could consist of just one or two people. You must first consider your goal and the resources you will need to accomplish it. Lay out all the steps it will take to get it done and then assign people to the areas where you need their support. Note these two examples: writing a book versus starting a dog walking company.

Whether you are starting a small business or writing a book, applying for school or losing fifteen pounds, there are a series of steps that you must take in order to accomplish that goal. Some steps you can do independently, but other steps require you to collaborate with others. Trying to do everything alone will only lead to burnout or feelings of isolation.

| Writing a Book | Starting a Dog Walking Company |
|---|---|
| Determine an area of focus | Establish a name |
| Set a deadline | Legalize your business |
| Make a writing schedule | Get insurance and complete paperwork |
| Find an editor | Create an activity program |
| Create a support network (prayer and accountability partners) | Create a support network (prayer and accountability partners) |
| Find a graphic designer | Create business cards & website |
| Find a publisher | Obtain supplies for your business |
| Develop a marketing team | Find clients |
| Launch | Launch |

Making a list of the people who will help you at each step of the journey will give you a sense of support from the very beginning of the process. Knowing that you have people in your corner who can help you along the way will alleviate the burden of carrying the weight of your goal alone.

Team members may consist of family members and friends, or they may be other professionals who have the expertise you lack and require for your project to be successful. Don't be intimidated by the word *team*. Some teams meet regularly and are very interactive, while other teams never meet in person, but rather communicate via telephone, email, and other communication mediums. It is important to note that your confidence will grow stronger when you aren't the only one pushing for your dream to be accomplished.

> Having people who believe in you and support you is a great source of motivation.

Having people who believe in you and support you is a great source of motivation. It's easy to start off with a bang, but once things get rolling and you start facing challenges discouragement can quickly set in, making it difficult to press on. This is where a supportive network comes in. The assistance you receive from your team can go a long way as a source of encouragement.

When I planned my very first women's conference in 2010, I was blessed to have the entire event downloaded right into my heart. I knew exactly how many sessions there would be, the title of the keynote sessions, and the feel of the day from start to finish. Once I wrote all those pieces down and made a clear map of how the day would go, I shared the idea with my husband and my friend, Adrienne. Thankfully, she caught the vision and jumped right on board. My husband plans major events in his sleep, so he was also in support of me moving forward. If the conference was just going to be the three of us, we would have been ready to go, but I had to reach out to more than just those two people.

I envisioned having a successful event and dialogued with God about it, but I hesitated when it came to sharing it with anyone else. Though it all seemed sensible, taking the leap of faith and sharing my heart with others meant that I was at risk of being rejected, ridiculed, criticised, and judged. I didn't want to put myself at risk of receiving all those things. However, I also realized that if I was going to attain my goal I would have to walk through the scary places of criticism, judgement, and rejection.

The bottom-line is we can't do what we dream about doing alone; we need people to help and support us along the way. I knew how to talk, encourage, and empower women, but I didn't know how to source out sponsors, engage in marketing, and take care of décor. So if my event was going to be successful I would need to ask for help from the people I knew. One by one, I picked up the phone and filled in the gaps that I could not fill myself. My team was made up of friends, family, and even some people I didn't know that well. Building a team worked, and through the conference I accomplished exactly what I felt God had called me to do.

Over the years, we've had eight successful conferences, and several other smaller women's events. The team hasn't stayed the same, and it hasn't always been easy working with other people. I've often struggled with the allure of simply working alone, but year after year I'm faced with the same reality—*teamwork makes the dream work.* I've decided that I prefer to be successful over comfortable, so I allow God to lead me to the right people and I rely on Him to show me how to lead my support team towards the goal.

**Benefits of Having a Strong Team**

*Support*

Knowing that you have someone who can be of assistance to you is sometimes all you need to keep pressing on to the end. If you're anything like me, you might find it a bit challenging to ask for help, but once you accept that you're not a superhero it becomes easier to admit that you do need support. Ask God to lead you to the right people to receive the help you need. It could be the person who's willing to proofread the content for your website, or the friend who will babysit your kids long enough for you to get a couple of tasks done. Sometimes all you need is to know that people are willing to offer their support should you need it. My husband is not a writer, and many times he's not able to contribute to what I'm working on because I desire a female perspective. However, as a night owl I do most of my work after the kids are fast asleep, so much of his support comes in the form of just lying on the couch, keeping me company while I type away in silence, exchanging a joke or a comment here or there.

*Encouragement*

Encouragement can come in the form of words or acts of service that people can do to let us know they want to see us win. A card, a few words or prayer over the phone, an open ear to offer feedback on the ideas we're sorting through, whatever it may be for you, be sure to treasure all you get. After spending time with my encouragers, I usually feel inspired. I am always reminded that God really called me to do the things I'm working so diligently to accomplish.

We all need people in our lives who believe in us and encourage us with their words and actions. Encouragers have the ability to motivate us when inspiration is running low, and they can do so with both their words and deeds. So be alert and recognize those who have been placed in your life to encourage you.

*Accountability*

Who are the people that hold you to task on the things you have committed yourself to complete? When you make a declaration, for example, "I want to lose ten pounds," who can you count on to help ensure that you stay on course?

We all need people in our lives who challenge us and hold us to the things we say we want to do. It can be frustrating at times, but we all need accountability partners in our lives. It is just too easy to let our deadlines and goals slip when we are the only ones who know about them.

**How to Develop Your Support Team**

When you write out the steps to achieving your goal (as in the table above) there will be some blanks. You will likely be responsible for the bulk of what must be done, but you can't do everything on your own.

> Be intentional about surrounding yourself with encouragers throughout the process.

Begin by listing what and who is missing (tasks you don't know how to do and those things you need help with). Don't forget to include areas for encouragement, prayer, and accountability.

Start by considering who is currently in your corner, the people who are already cheering you along in life. It could be family members, very close friends, or people who really like and admire you. Don't minimize the importance of having genuine words of encouragement from people who care about you. There are times when you will lose faith in yourself and doubt if you can truly accomplish your goals. Those are the times when your cheerleaders are most needed. Don't wait till all hope is lost and you're about to throw in the towel to receive encouragement. Be intentional about surrounding yourself with encouragers throughout the process and let people know that their role on the team is to help you stay motivated and encouraged.

Next, look for people who have the skills you require. If finances are limited, then seek out people who are looking for an opportunity to use their skills. When I was planning my first conference I needed someone to help me seek out sponsorship. My husband had a friend with a background in fundraising who was unemployed at the time, so I reached out to her and explained that my budget was limited and told her what I could afford to pay her for her services and she agreed.

Finally, list the services you will have to retain from a professional and see how their expertise fits into making your goal a reality. You may be the mastermind behind your goal, but if it's a new venture, it would make sense for you to consider allowing others who have some experience in the field to influence you in a positive way.

## Mentors

A mentor is a trusted individual who can counsel and guide you in the decisions you must make. Ideally, it should be someone who is ahead of you on their journey, whether in age, spiritual maturity, or professional development. It should be someone you can look up to and seek out for guidance on how to go about your pursuits.

Who do you have in your life that influences you in a positive way and pushes you closer to your goal? It could be a teacher, a counsellor, a pastor, or a supervisor. God has placed people in your life to pour into you. You cannot expect to grow alone; you need the support of others to help you develop into all that God has called you to be. God works through people to accomplish His work, so find those who have opened themselves up to be used by God in your life.

Everyone has their own path. While I would discourage anyone from trying to copy another person's exact steps for getting to a particular destination, there are a lot of lessons that we can all learn from other people's journey. It's good to learn from others' experiences, but it is impractical to redo everything they've done, exactly the way they've done it. Being a copycat is never a good idea, unless you're copying Jesus, of course.

Don't forget the ones God uses from afar. I have said for years that I view Joyce Meyer as my own personal mentor. I've never met her in person and have only seen her minister twice in real life. However, I have soaked myself in her teachings via her television ministry and her books. Although I don't know her personally, I have found that God has used her words to encourage, convict, and instruct me in so many areas of my life—marriage, motherhood, ministry, and my personal walk with the Lord. I have seen how God has used the stories she shares as well as her style to help me mature, and I'm so thankful for her ministry.

## Research

Once you've listed the preliminary steps to fulfilling your goal and you've identified the gaps, you may need to do some research to help you fill in whatever is missing. You may need to take a course, interview other professionals within your desired field, or go online to explore what is available. It is amazing how much information is accessible online. I recall being at a dental appointment to be treated for a horrendous toothache and the dentist prescribed a particular antibiotic for me to take. I questioned him on whether it was safe for me to take while still breastfeeding my son and, to my surprise, he turned around to his computer and Googled it. I was shocked because although that is what I would have done, I expected him to log onto a medical site that I wouldn't have access to. That experience helped to remind me that information is available to all of us, regardless of our educational background, as long as we are willing to look for it.

## Outsourcing

A friend once told me that whenever she needs something done at home that she's not able to do herself, like fixing something complex, she speaks to her husband and asks him to get it looked after. If he takes a longer time than what seems reasonable, she will give him a warning that she's going to look into outsourcing the job to a professional, which will

> Don't hesitate to outsource for the help you don't already have.

end up costing them. Then, if more time passes, she will go ahead and call a professional in to help solve the problem.

There are times when accomplishing the task will require you to outsource and get assistance from someone that isn't necessarily on your team, yet they become essential to your success because you just don't have the resources to do it without them. Don't hesitate to outsource for the help you don't already have. It will likely cost you, so prepare for that, and remember that your dream is worth investing in. If finances are a concern, then remember that God is the author of the vision He placed it in your heart, and as such you can ask Him for the resources you need to bring the dream to life.

# Key Questions
## Step 3: Supporting Cast

1. Who are the people and what are the resources that you need to help you get to your destination?
2. Do you have people on your team who fill the roles of supporter, encourager, and accountability partner?
3. Where are the gaps in your team?

# Prayer

Dear Lord, I thank you for the people you have placed in my life. I realize that you can use all my experiences and encounters, both good and bad, to shape me into the person you've called me to be. Will you please open my eyes to see the relationships that you have ordained for this time in my life? Help me take good care of these relationships and help me foster all the other relationships that you are bringing to me to help me during this time of my life. Show me the people I need to avoid and the relationships that are steering me away from your plan for my life. Please reveal to me the resources I will need moving forward and the resources I may have overlooked.

Amen

# Chapter 7
# Step 4: Building a Timeline for Success

Time is a valuable commodity. Deanna Wadsworth once said, "Four things you can't recover—the stone after the throw, the word after it's said, the occasion after it's missed, and the time after it's gone."

**The Importance of Time**

Treasure your time for it is a blessing. Each moment we have been given is a gift and we should treat it as such. We begin the journey of life not knowing how much time we have on earth. Oftentimes, we take for granted that we'll be here indefinitely, we get comfortable, focus on our enjoyment, and live a carefree life. It isn't until we hit some crisis—we lose a loved one, a health issue pops up, or we realize we're getting older—that we face the reality that we don't have all the time in the world at our disposal. Every day we wake up is an opportunity to do something great.

Unfortunately, although it seems easy to make time for other people's needs, we often don't make time for our own personal goals. Therefore, it is important to have a plan for what we will accomplish in the twenty-four hours we've been given each day. It is better to do this before we start the day. For an even more effective plan, each Sunday map out what your week will look like in detail.

Being a mother of three young children and working full-time is not an easy task. I find that being "Mom" alone is enough to keep my daily schedule full to the max. I often wonder how much simpler life would be if I only focused on being a mom. I sometimes daydream about the idea, but the truth is that I have a very strong call on my life to use my gifts as a psychotherapist and a communicator to help and support others along their life journey. I am also called to be the best mom and wife I can be to my family.

Shortly after having my first son, I came to the realization that I prefer the kind of mom that I am when I am able to express all the facets of myself as a person, as opposed to focusing solely on being a mom. When I get a chance to see my clients, to speak at an event, or plan an empowering women's workshop, I come home to my family with excitement and a sense of fulfillment.

Nevertheless, as a working mother my plate is full and it's very easy to become overwhelmed with too much to do. Therefore, it is essential that I plan out very carefully how my time will be spent.

## How Are You Using Your Time?

Most of us wake up in the morning and before our feet hit the ground we find ourselves doing multiple things. We check our smart phones, our e-mail inboxes, and our social media accounts. Then, before we know it, time has flown by and we're rushing out the door to get to work or school. I have often started my day with the intention to accomplish this, that, and the other, but then I get to the end of the day and I'm amazed at how little I actually accomplished on my to-do list. Usually I wonder where all the time went, but the truth is if you do not assign your time, your time will assign itself. If you don't make a plan for how your day should go and attach lengths of time to your schedule, it is very likely that you may never get around to accomplishing what you were hoping to get done.

Have you ever considered how the time you thought you once had has slipped through your fingertips? You will soon discover that time has a way of wasting away before you realize it is happening. My definition of wasted time is *time that could have been used for your benefit but was spent accomplishing nothing of value.*

The word *benefit* doesn't mean that only the time you use to do things for yourself is time well spent. In fact, spending time with someone in need is not only beneficial to others, but also benefits you immensely. You are the best judge of what benefits you. It is sometimes hard to pinpoint what is beneficial to us, but we all know how it feels to have wasted time. Making the best use of your time starts by recognizing how you are currently using your time. How efficient are you with your time? If you had to rate yourself on how well you use your time, what would your score be?

Begin by keeping a time log to track your daily activities. It may seem daunting, but this is the first step to making the best use of your time. Completing a time log will allow you to see where you are most productive throughout your day, where there are open spots for the activities you need to focus more time on, and the unhelpful patterns you may be engaging in that are wasting your time.

Simple example of a time log that can be used daily:

| | Sun | Mon | Tues | Wed | Thurs | Fri | Sat |
|---|---|---|---|---|---|---|---|
| A | | | | | | | |
| C | | | | | | | |
| T | | | | | | | |
| I | | | | | | | |
| V | | | | | | | |
| I | | | | | | | |
| T | | | | | | | |
| Y | | | | | | | |
| | | | | | | | |
| T | | | | | | | |
| I | | | | | | | |
| M | | | | | | | |
| E | | | | | | | |
| | | | | | | | |
| L | | | | | | | |
| O | | | | | | | |
| G | | | | | | | |

Commit to completing a time log for a typical week. Don't jot down how you *think* you spent your time or how you *intended* to spend your time, but rather how you actually spent your time. It's best to keep your time log close at hand and fill it in every hour or every time you switch tasks.

> The fact of the matter is we are not guaranteed any amount of time, no matter how talented, young, healthy, strong, or ambitious we are.

Once you've taken the time to complete your time log, try to identify how you have been wasting your time. Also identify areas where you've been efficient in getting things done.

Learning to maximize your time requires becoming aware of the unhelpful habits that get in the way of maximizing your time. Everyone has their own struggles, but some of the most common habits that steal our time are:

*Forgetting that time waits for no one*

I remember having a conversation with a friend in my teenage years. She said, "I know that I need to be living my life for God, but I'm young, and there is too much for me to do right now. I will eventually make that commitment to God when I'm a lot older." How many times do you remember making a statement like that? Knowing that you are supposed to do something, but assuming that you'll have time to do it later, as if you are guaranteed all the time in the world. The fact of the matter is we are not guaranteed any amount of time, no matter how talented, young, healthy, strong, or ambitious we are. That young teenage girl is now a woman, and if given the opportunity to talk about her adolescence, she would share that there were many decisions that she ended up making that she now regrets. She was blessed with time, but she missed opportunities she will never get back because time does not stand still.

*Spending too much time on unhelpful things*

It amazes me how much time we spend entertaining ourselves on a daily basis. Things like social media, television, movies, dining out, and shopping are just a few of the things we spend too much of our time on. While there is a time and place for these pleasures, we often spend more time pleasuring ourselves than improving ourselves.

Apart from the time you spend at work, school, or sleeping, consider what you spend most of your time doing. Are you making the best use of your time? Are the things you do helpful?

*Focusing on feeling good*

We live in a culture where we are told that if something doesn't feel good, then we don't need to endure it. Not only are we self-centred and self-focused, we are also obsessed with feeling good. We set goals because they feel like good goals to achieve, but we forget to count the cost necessary to actualize them.

We hardly allow ourselves to sit through things that make us feel uncomfortable or that result in strain. So much so that we end up doing only what we feel like doing. Today we may feel like working out, but tomorrow we may not, so we put our goal aside until we feel like doing what is required. It's sad to know that we've allowed ourselves to become so undisciplined that we allow our emotions and feelings to determine our actions. Being led by our feelings always leads to stagnation. Progress requires strain, frustration, discomfort, and sometimes even pain. There is no shortcut to success; we must put in the time in order to get the prize.

**How to Restore Lost Time**

*Confess*

No one enjoys admitting when they are wrong. It's hard looking at ourselves and seeing our flaws and how they have hurt us and others, still we must learn the discipline of admitting when we've done wrong. Only then can the Lord begin to help us to change for the better.

Confession doesn't have to be a drawn out, painful experience. It's as simple as saying "Lord, I've done it again. I've messed up and I'm sorry." God already knows you've messed up, but He wants you to humble yourself and acknowledge your sin.

There isn't a soul alive that hasn't made the mistake of wasting time. We do it without thinking, so there's no use beating yourself up about it. Acknowledge the areas in which you lack good time-management and commit your time back to God.

*Turn away*

When you humble yourself and acknowledge where you have misused the time God has given you, and you recommit your time back to Him, He will respond to you. If you are unsure of other areas where you might be misusing your time, bring it up in prayer and God will reveal what He wants you to know and He will show you the areas that you need to change.

God will use the Holy Spirit to show you how He wants you to use your time for Him; and once He does so, it is your job to turn away from the old habits He has revealed to you. The Holy Spirit will lead and direct you each day and let you know if what you're doing is in line with God's will or out of step with His plan for your life. It may be a feeling you get when you're doing a project, or something a person says that resonates within you.

God does not expect you to figure things out on your own, nor does He expect that you will make the necessary changes on your own. The truth is you are unable to do the work that must be done inside of you, and that is why you must rely on the Holy Spirit. He will empower you to do what God wants you to do; all you need to focus on is turning away from the old things that held you back.

*Run towards*

Breaking habits seem hard at first, but they won't be as hard if you replace them with new habits and behaviours that lead you in a more helpful direction. As God reveals to you the things you do daily that steal your time, He will also reveal to you the things that will make better use of your time. Perhaps there is a comfortable way of doing a task that you are used to doing, but God impresses upon your heart to stop doing the task that way. When God shows you a different way, you will be surprised at how your obedience results in you having more time than you expected.

Turning away is the next step after confession. As you turn away from the thing that was getting in your way, you must turn towards God and chase after the things of God with all your heart. There will never be a point in your life when you don't have something to pursue with God. As long as you're alive, He has something that He wants to do in you. This is why we must continually focus on God and actively pursue Him with all our heart, mind, and soul.

When we truly commit our time to God, all his purposes for us will be fulfilled in our lives. You may have wasted time in the past, but I promise you that if you turn away from your old, sinful ways today and run towards God, He will restore the time that was lost and fulfil His purpose for your life. Joel 2:25 tells us that God can and will restore the time that the locust has stolen from you. Turn to Him and allow Him to prove Himself in your life.

**Organizing Your Time**

Don't become overwhelmed with all you have to accomplish. Break down the goal into areas you can focus on weekly; then break the week down into days. Don't try to get it all done because you won't and will just end up feeling defeated. Start with one focus per week and then keep adding as you gain consistency. The mapping process involves scheduling what you need to do from day one till the deadline. Every single day, week, and month we have goals that need to be clearly spelled out and put into our timeline.

**Timeline**

Your timeline can be built once you have laid out your goal. The purpose of the timeline is to help you work backwards and detail all the items that must be done in order to successfully achieve the final goal. You may build it into your agenda, your smart phone, a notebook, or on your computer, whatever works best for you. Each day, week, or month, set mini-goals that act as steps to accomplishing your ultimate goal.

As you lay out your life map, assign dates and times to meet with mentors and people who are equipped to assist or support you. Practise journaling and holding yourself accountable to avoiding things that have gotten in the way in the past. Do things that keep you motivated and inspired, and keep a checklist of the things that are getting done. Keep a running worksheet of

> You need to pace yourself and be intentional about what it is that you are doing as you work towards accomplishing your goals.

where you are on your journey every single month, what you're doing, and the ideas you want to pursue in the near future along with the timelines you've assigned to these ideas.

For example, if I'm a writer and I am currently working on developing a blog, I need to have a system in place to regularly publish my pieces. I also need to be consistent with this process so that I can get everything done in a timely manner. After consistently writing my blog for several months, I may add writing a book to my plate. The point is not to become overwhelmed by our ideas and the potential that is within us. We need to have a plan in place for what we are trying to accomplish. Also, avoid feeling a sense of jealousy or envy when it comes to what others are doing. Don't feel the need to do, right now, what someone else is doing. Pace yourself and be intentional about what it is that you are doing as you work towards accomplishing your goals.

A time management schedule can be formally defined as a representation or exhibit of key events arranged chronologically. Writing a map is comparable to making a list for going to the grocery store or laying out from the night before the clothes and all the things you'll need the next day. When you go to the grocery store with that list, you can navigate through your shopping experience a lot faster than the person who just went with the intention of

*Example of a Weekly Time Management Sheet:*

|        | Sun | Mon | Tues | Wed | Thurs | Fri | Sat |
|--------|-----|-----|------|-----|-------|-----|-----|
| 8:00   |     |     |      |     |       |     |     |
| 9:00   |     |     |      |     |       |     |     |
| 10:00  |     |     |      |     |       |     |     |
| 11:00  |     |     |      |     |       |     |     |
| 12:00  |     |     |      |     |       |     |     |
| 1:00   |     |     |      |     |       |     |     |
| 2:00   |     |     |      |     |       |     |     |
| 3:00   |     |     |      |     |       |     |     |
| 4:00   |     |     |      |     |       |     |     |
| 5:00   |     |     |      |     |       |     |     |
| 6:00   |     |     |      |     |       |     |     |
| 7:00   |     |     |      |     |       |     |     |
| 8:00   |     |     |      |     |       |     |     |
| 9:00   |     |     |      |     |       |     |     |

picking up whatever they can remember. With the list, you'll be able to ensure that you get all the items you need, and you are less likely to steer off course by getting things you don't actually need. Similarly, when you prepare from the night before, it helps your morning to flow so much smoother. We can all relate to getting up in the morning, knowing we have somewhere to go and thinking, "I'm really tired. I just want to go back to sleep." But if you take that extra couple of minutes to put your bags, your kids' bags, and everything else you're going to need together the night before, it will make your morning go a lot smoother; in fact, you may even have time to spare.

## How to Remain Faithful to Your Timeline

Hebrews 12:11 says, "No discipline seems pleasant at the time, but painful. Later on, however, it produces a harvest of righteousness and peace for those who have been trained by it." (NIV)

*Embrace the struggle*

Recognize that it will be a struggle at times to stay committed to your timeline. It would be easier to just 'go with the flow' and do what feels natural to you. However, this wouldn't help you to accomplish your goals. In the long run, you will end up mismanaging your time and losing sight of the bottom line. I would love to tell you that it was going to be easy knowing that you have this great goal waiting to greet you at the end, but unfortunately, that isn't usually enough to keep us faithful to our timeline. Our nature is to resist it and to go back to old habits and use our time to do whatever we typically find ourselves doing.

Therefore, prepare yourself to feel some resistance. It may not come in the beginning, but it may come a week or two into following your timeline. Perhaps you'll get tired of taking the time to plan out your week and become tempted to simply repeat what you've been doing for the past while. Whatever the circumstance, struggle will present itself and will always challenge your desire to stick with your plan.

*Form the habit*

How many days does it take for you to form a habit? Seven? Twenty-one? Thirty? Whatever the length of time, focus on forming the habits necessary to accomplish your goals. Thinking about the weeks, months, and even years it will take to get you to your goal can make anyone cry defeat prematurely. If you aren't careful, you can get to a place where you want to see results so desperately that you become discouraged. Always remember that consistency is the thing that will bring you across the finish line; simply doing what is required, day in and day out. Whenever you get to a point where you're frustrated by how long it's taking to see results or to get to the finish line, simply concentrate on what you need to get done that day.

*No need for perfection*

Faithfulness isn't defined by perfection or never making mistakes. Faithfulness is determined by what you do once you've fallen down. Will you pick yourself up and get back on track with what you have committed to do? Or will you stay down and give up on your commitment completely?

> God is not looking for perfection from us because we would all be hopeless.

Thankfully, God is not looking for perfection from us, or else we would all be hopeless. God realizes that we are incapable of doing half the things we set out to do. That's why He sent us His son to be all that we need and to help us do all that we need to do.

Being faithful to your timeline and to your life map isn't going to happen because you didn't make mistakes, it will happen because you allowed God to show you how to be faithful with the gift of purpose He has placed inside of you.

*Keep the end in mind*

Never lose sight of your goal or your sense of purpose that connects you to your goals. It's easy to get bogged down with the stress of what needs to get done instead of focusing on the reasons why you're doing the things that need to be done.

By writing your life map you plan for where you want to land. Once you've established your goal, you can move backwards and consider what you need to accomplish each step of the way. People don't like to think about the end; however, I believe that doing so helps to put our daily activities into perspective. We tend to appreciate things more once we realize that they won't last forever. Therefore, live with the end in mind.

# Key Questions
## Step 4: Building a Timeline for Success

1. How do you spend your time on a daily basis?
2. What are the unhelpful things and activities that steal your time?
3. Have you created a timeline for accomplishing your goal(s)?

# Prayer

Thank you for this day, Lord. Thank you for the days you have allowed me to see thus far. I don't think I've truly appreciated the time you've blessed me with up to this point. Lord, I don't want to waste any more time. Please show me how to use my time more efficiently, so that my purpose in life can be fulfilled. I want to please you with how I spend the time you have blessed me with daily. Help me understand this gift of time and help me increase in wisdom as I create a timeline for the days that lie ahead.

Amen

# Chapter 8
# Step 5: Preparing for Barriers and Roadblocks

When I think about barriers, I think of this short story, written by Portia Nelson, that I heard several years ago.

**There's a Hole in My Sidewalk** (© Portia Nelson)

*Chapter One*

I walk down the street.

There is a deep hole in the sidewalk.

I fall in.

I am lost... I am helpless.

It isn't my fault.

It takes forever to find a way out.

*Chapter Two*

I walk down the same street.

There is a deep hole in the sidewalk.

I pretend I don't see it.

I fall in again.

I can't believe I am in the same place.

But it isn't my fault.

It still takes a long time to get out.

*Chapter Three*

I walk down the same street.

There is a deep hole in the sidewalk.

I see it is there.

I still fall in... it's a habit.

My eyes are open.

I know where I am.

It is my fault... I get out immediately.


*Chapter Four*

I walk down the same street.

There is a deep hole in the sidewalk.

I walk around it.


Chapter Five

I walk down another street.


I love reading and sharing this story because I believe there is so much that we can learn from it. It speaks of the loss of innocence, the difficulties and challenges in life, the distressing feelings, the sense of self-discovery and self-awareness, wisdom, empowerment, and finally, change!

Who can't relate to having barriers in their life? Only the person who is oblivious to the world around them can honestly say that they have no barriers. But for the rest of us that are trying to accomplish something with our lives, it is inevitable that we will face barriers and obstacles throughout our journey.

Barriers are the things that get in your way; the things that slow you down—a hiccup, a roadblock that is sitting between where you are and where you want to be. Barriers are the things that threaten your success in accomplishing your goals. A barrier can be as simple as the flu that stops you from getting to the gym for a week, or the realization that you have to go back to school to qualify for the promotion you are going for at work. It can be something as trivial as missing the bus, or something more devastating like the loss of a job. Regardless of how big or how small, barriers bring about the same result; they keep you away from your goal.

No one likes barriers, but we can all anticipate experiencing them. In fact, it's impossible to live life without encountering many roadblocks along the way. The journey of life is not a straight path; there are dips and turns and many roadblocks that slow down our progress. Failing to expect them will further slow us down, so be prepared for when they occur.

How can you best prepare for your roadblocks? I believe that you can prepare for roadblocks by imagining some of the things that *could* go wrong. One way to do this is by looking at how other people who've pursued a similar goal have struggled along the way. You cannot guarantee that the same roadblocks they experienced will be the same things you will go through, but you can learn from their experiences. Start by imagining how you might have dealt with a particular issue that they had to face.

Another thing to remember about roadblocks is that many times you won't see them until they are right in front of your face. That is because they often come without warning. You could be expecting things to go one way, and may have taken all the right steps to ensure that they do, yet something completely out of your control pops up and throws a wrench into your plans. It seems hard to plan for things that are unanticipated, but you can help yourself be better prepared by working diligently on being in a healthy place, both mentally and emotionally.

There is no way to know exactly what is waiting around the bend in the road, but it is safe to say that you must remain alert, knowing that roadblocks are imminent.

Roadblocks don't always look like a big boulder in the road or a huge stop sign that forces you to come to a jolting halt. Roadblocks sometimes look like distractions; they appear to be little frustrations but, if left unaddressed, will take you off course and leave you feeling unable to go on.

*The journey of life is not a straight path; there are dips and turns and many roadblocks that slow down our progress.*

**Three Steps to Successfully Navigate Around Roadblocks**

*Focus on the BIG picture*

It's easy to lose sight of the big picture when you're dealing with the issues that arise within the smaller areas of your goal. This is where your mission and vision statements come in handy. If your goal is to support people in your community using your skills as an artist, and you're working on a major event and experiencing hiccups along the way, remember that your goal is not to be the best event planner ever, but rather to share your art.

Roadblocks have a way of causing us to lose focus on the most important thing—our bottom line. At the beginning of your life map journey you would have written out your purpose for pursuing your goal; keep it close throughout the process. Whenever your roadblocks present themselves, remember that your purpose remains the same, and therefore you still have a job to do.

*Prioritize*

When you face challenges, there tends to be more than one thing to attend to. It may sometimes become overwhelming trying to figure out what to address first. Don't allow the anxiety to slow you down; instead, make a list of the things that need to get done and figure out which tasks must be completed first to allow the other steps to flow smoothly. Ask yourself, "What do I need to do now?" If you're finding it hard to focus due to being overly-stressed, then invite someone on your support team to brainstorm ideas with you. Allow them to help you organize your list of priorities.

*Keep moving*

Always remember that in spite of the roadblocks that get in your way, you must still forge on. Keep your eye on the prize and proceed! It's okay to take a moment to catch your breath, but ensure that whatever you do is properly calculated. Rest, regrouping, and self-care are not just things that happen after big projects are accomplished; they need to be included in your timeline to help prevent you from burning out. Also, remember that dealing with roadblocks shouldn't be deemed as getting off track. Roadblocks are not odd phenomena on our journey, they are inevitable parts of the process. Expect them, do what you can to prepare for them, and then, using the wisdom God has given you, carefully deal with them and move on.

Life is full of obstacles, so how can we use them to motivate us? Some obstacles are self-created and others are completely outside of our control. Sometimes we make mistakes due to our poor judgment or our inexperience, and we end up experiencing obstacles as a result. These obstacles are usually easier to face once we take ownership for our actions and decide to make a change.

The obstacles that are caused due to other people or circumstances out of our control can sometimes be a lot harder to contend with. Although obstacles are to be expected, they can cause much frustration, especially when there seems to be no way of changing the circumstances right away. What are some of the obstacles that you have faced in your life? How have you been able to overcome these barriers?

Always ensure that you are aware of your mental and emotional state as this will affect how much motivation and energy you have to resolve the problem. How you react to the obstacle can also help or hinder how well you get past it. How do you typically react to obstacles in your life? Does the way you typically react to obstacles help or hinder you?

> Remember that in spite of the roadblocks that get in your way, you must still forge on.

Don't make the mistake of thinking that obstacles are only there to get in your way; there are so many things that can be gained from obstacles if you shift your mindset towards them. Obstacles bring opportunities with them—opportunities for us to grow, opportunities for us to try new and different things, and opportunities to change directions when necessary. A large part of successfully navigating around our obstacles is beginning to appreciate what the obstacle brings us.

Appreciating our obstacles starts when we ask these questions:

- o What is the function of the obstacle?
- o How is this obstacle helpful for me?
- o How will I mature after getting through this?

While everything that we go through isn't always pleasant, it's possible that even the unpleasant things can help to make us better. For example, a health crisis can force you to change your lifestyle and choose to become healthier. Or lack of support can cause you to recognize your need for more supportive people in your life, which in turn may lead you to go out and develop healthier relationships.

Obstacles have the ability to frustrate, discourage, confuse, and even leave us feeling hopeless, but the reality is that when we feel these unpleasant emotions they can bring us to our knees. When we get to a place where our backs are against the wall and we are out of options, we have a choice—we can either hold our hands up in the air and cry defeat, or we can hold our heads up to heaven and cry out to God for help. When we are on our knees, we are at a place of complete humility where we recognize that we don't have all the answers and we aren't self-reliant. It is also here that we have an opportunity to grow our faith in God.

In 2 Corinthians 12:7-10, Paul talks about the thorn in his side:

> So to keep me from becoming proud, I was given a thorn in my flesh, a messenger from Satan to torment me and keep me from becoming proud. Three different times I begged the Lord to take it away. Each time he said, "My grace is all you need. My power works best in weakness." So now I am glad to boast about my weaknesses, so that the power of Christ can work through me. That's why I take pleasure in my weaknesses and in the insults,

*hardships, persecutions, and troubles that I suffer*
*for Christ. For when I am weak, then I am strong.*

In this passage Paul shares the difficult things he experienced during his walk with God. The great things he did for God did not exempt him from dealing with his own obstacles. He referred to it as a thorn in his flesh that had a dual purpose. Paul said that this thorn both tormented him and helped him at the same time, in that it kept him

from becoming proud. After praying for it to be taken away, he finally came to realize the function of the obstacle. The fact is our obstacles, struggles, challenges, failures, and distresses are meant to bring us to our knees. Once on our knees, we have a choice, we can either allow ourselves to become overcome by the crisis and stay stuck, or we can look up and cry out to the Saviour for help.

As crazy as it may seem, your struggles are a vehicle that God uses to make you stronger. You may not feel strong while you are in the struggle, but if you humble yourself and confess how much you need your heavenly Father's help, He will step in and cause you to experience strength beyond your imagination. Therefore, the trials you face actually end up making you a stronger person.

"Consider it pure joy, my brothers and sisters, whenever you face trials of many kinds, because you know that the testing of your faith produces perseverance. Let perseverance finish its work so that you may be mature and complete, not lacking anything." (James 1:2-4)

When you allow God to minister to you during your struggles, He will ensure that you rise up in victory.

**What Can Your Obstacles Teach You?**

*Reality Check*

The world is in chaos. Just watch the evening news. Whenever I watch the news, I have to mentally talk myself out of feeling anxious about the state of the world. There is so much crime that it almost seems hopeless. We live in a sinful world that has, for the most part, turned its back on God. When we face the reality of the troubles in our world, we are reminded that we are here for a purpose. Being here on earth isn't primarily about having a good time, or achieving great heights personally, professionally, and socially. We have a purpose to be a light that shines in the darkness around us (Matthew 5:16).

When we face our obstacles, it reminds us of our purpose. Our hardship very quickly knocks the rose-coloured glasses off our face and forces us to see things as they really are. When we allow the Holy Spirit to lead us He shows us that our obstacles point back to the reality of our ultimate purpose. Our reality check is a wakeup call that in our own strength we cannot accomplish much, but when we focus on God and allow Him to lead us, we can succeed in all we do.

*Our Limitations*

God has placed purpose inside of everyone and has given us all an assignment to carry out with our lives. It is exciting whenever we initially discover that sense of purpose and feel the adrenaline pumping through our veins. After some time, however, we naturally become weary. We encounter obstacles, challenges, rejection, and disappointments. We experience failure due to the mistakes we make and we begin to question our abilities and doubt if we can really accomplish what we've set out to do. The truth is that we are frail at our very core, and so if it were up to our own strength and know-how, we would be unable to do half the things we set out to accomplish throughout our lives. When we come up against obstacles, such as being fired, being rejected for a promotion, being criticized, or being denied access to something important, it is a bitter reminder of our limitations.

It is easy to deny the truth that our limitations are significant and that we are unable to accomplish our goals on our own. It is easy to deny these things because we live in a world that tries to sell us the illusion of 'empowerment' and 'inner-strength.' Those beliefs may motivate you for a while, but on their own they cannot bring you to the finish line successfully. The only way you're going to make it to the finish line is by admitting that you have limitations and that you need to reach outside of yourself in order to finish strong.

> The only way you're going to make it to the finish line is by admitting that you have limitations and that you need to reach outside of yourself in order to finish strong.

*Our Dependence*

No one is an island. Too often we take on the mentality of being a lone soldier. But I've never heard of a soldier going to war alone. Soldiers are a part of a unit that enters into an assignment together. Each soldier relies on his counterparts to help accomplish the mission. So don't be confused; we all need each other. Our family, friends, colleagues, and co-labourers are all individuals we will need to lean on during some part of our journey. Many people hate feeling that they are dependent on others. However, the ones who recognize this truth have the benefit of maximizing their relationships and achieving success quicker than those who try to 'soldier' it alone.

*How to Overcome*

Our obstacles give us an opportunity to rise above our circumstances and become victorious. When we are faced with a road block, we can either confront it or run away from it. Our first instinct may be to give up, but if we stand our ground, our obstacles give us the opportunity to experience victory. Without obstacles we would never have the opportunity to exercise our survival skills.

It has been said that anything worth having is worth fighting for, so if you're working on something that has worth, be prepared to fight for that thing and fight hard. You overcome when you continue to fight until you've passed that obstacle. Without that obstacle sitting in front of you, you would never experience what it feels like to get around it. It's a good feeling once you've overcome and seen your challenges defeated, so don't give up!

**Practical Steps for Overcoming**

1. *Guard your heart*

"Above all else, guard your heart, for everything you do flows from it." (Proverbs 4:23)

Consider your heart as the main artery for the highway to your life. When your heart is hurt, heavy, or broken, all aspects of your life will be negatively affected. Many times people have issues of the heart, and they try to ignore the pain and put on a mask to avoid dealing with it. Unfortunately, we've been created in such a way that we can't hide the issues of our heart for long.

Whether it's your job, your relationships, or your health, whatever's impacting your heart will spill out and reveal itself in the other areas of your life. Learning to guard your heart requires that you first submit your mind, thoughts, and actions to God. Biblically speaking, the heart is the totality of who we are inside: our emotions, our intellect, our desires, and our will.[1] It is therefore imperative that we mind the condition of our hearts, and if there are areas that need healing we should bring them to the Lord so He can minister healing to those areas.

When you come up against an obstacle, the issues of your heart will make it difficult for you to get around it. Instead of focusing on what God is saying, you will focus inward at your own struggles and miss receiving your breakthrough. The words we speak flow out of our hearts (Matthew 12:34), so it's imperative that we work diligently with the Lord to learn how to guard our hearts.

2.   *Guard your mouth*

"Set a guard over my mouth, Lord; keep watch over the door of my lips" (Palms 141:3). Your tongue carries the power of life and death (Proverbs 18:21). You have the ability to speak your way out of trouble, and you have the

---

[1] For more information on guarding your heart see:
http://marshill.com/2013/02/20/guard-your-heart

ability to speak yourself stuck. I remember being warned as a young child to be careful of what I say, but it was always in regards to not using my words to hurt other people's feelings. It wasn't until I grew up and began understanding more of the Bible that I understood that my words had more than the ability to hurt feelings, they could also bless me, curse me, build me up, or tear me down.

We often forget about the power that lies within our mouths. We tend to look for solutions everywhere else while forgetting that we can use our words to create the solutions we seek. Guarding your mouth will ensure that you use the power of your words to speak by faith over the things that aren't the way you need them to be. We must be mindful of what we say and be conscious of who we speak to because sometimes people can encourage words of discouragement and death during our difficult circumstances.

3.  *Renew your mind*

"Do not conform to the pattern of this world, but be transformed by the renewing of your mind. Then you will be able to test and approve what God's will is—his good, pleasing and perfect will." (Romans 12:2)

Our minds are connected to our thought life. Therefore, whatever we fill our minds with will end up consuming our thought life. If you fill your mind with garbage, then you can expect your thoughts to be filled with unhelpful beliefs and unhealthy ideologies that end up being harmful to you.

If you do not renew your mind, you will not have a good outlook when roadblocks present themselves. Renewing your mind happens when you consume the word of God daily. When you fill up on the truth, you will think truthful, positive, and empowering thoughts about the issues that may have otherwise thrown you off course.

When you allow God to show you how to guard your heart, your mouth, and your mind, you will be in a position to hear more clearly what the Lord is saying to you about your obstacles. Psalm 119:133 says, "Direct my footsteps according to your word; let no sin rule over me." When you ask God to direct your steps and not let sin rule over you, the next step is to stand on your faith and trust that He will do exactly as His word says.

God has His own way of dealing with things in our lives, and we need to approach Him and allow Him to resolve things the way He sees fit. So though you may initially imagine your problem being resolved one way, when you pray a prayer like David did in Psalm 119:133 and wait for God's leading, He may surprise you and do something you never even considered.

In the end, you must face your obstacles with faith and work diligently on not becoming anxious about the resolution of your obstacles. Philippians 4:6-9 is one of my favourite passages. God brings me back to that passage time and time again throughout my life. Although I've read it hundreds of times, it always grounds me and reminds me what to do if I lack peace and feel overwhelmed by a situation.

"Do not be anxious about anything, but in every situation, by prayer and petition, with thanksgiving, present your requests to God. And the peace of God, which transcends all understanding, will guard your hearts and your minds in Christ Jesus. Finally, brothers and sisters, whatever is true, whatever is noble, whatever is right, whatever is pure, whatever is lovely, whatever is admirable—if anything is excellent or praiseworthy—think about such things. Whatever you have learned or received or heard from me, or seen in me—put it into practice. And the God of peace will be with you." (Philippians 4:6-9)

# Key Questions
Step 5: Preparing for Barriers and Roadblocks

1. How do you typically react to obstacles in your life?

2. Does the way you typically react to obstacles help or hinder you?

3. What is the function of the obstacle you are facing?

4. How will you mature after getting through this?

# Prayer

Dear Lord, your word says that no weapon formed against me shall prosper. I realize that I have a very real enemy who is seeking to kill and destroy me as well as the purposes you have destined for my life. I realize that these tactics come as distractions and setbacks. Show me the areas that are being used to hold me back from where you are leading me, Lord. I am confident that I will have the victory as long as I continue to allow your Holy Spirit to lead me. As you fight each battle on my behalf, help me to just be still. I thank you, Lord, that you've already worked everything out for my good and I celebrate the fact that you will receive all the glory in my overcoming.

Amen

# Chapter 9
## Prepared for Success

Success isn't guaranteed; we must plan for it. The popular saying "failing to plan is planning to fail" can be applied to success. When we embark on a project, we need to ask ourselves the question, "What can I do to ensure that I am successful with this endeavour?"

Some goals will have an absolute definitive answer and others will not. Say, for example, a person has the goal of meeting the ideal partner, getting married, and starting a family, those things are subject to time and opportunity, among other things. Hence, it would be impossible to state exactly what needs to be done in order to experience success in that area. Other goals, however, do have clear and definitive targets, such as losing ten pounds or starting a website. Those goals are all attainable and within a person's control.

At this point, you should have your map clearly sketched out. You should have:

- A clear sense of your purpose

- Narrowed down the goal that you will be focusing on
- A timeline
- A list of people and resources for support
- A list of potential roadblocks

Now you need to prepare yourself for success. Success doesn't just happen on its own. It takes a series of calculated moves that are executed consistently over time. Success isn't when you get the

cheers and recognition for a job well done. Success happens when no one is paying attention to what you are doing, when no one is supporting or encouraging you, yet you press on anyhow and complete what you set out to do.

Something that will be very helpful for you to do is to include the question "What does success look like for me?" in your map. This will allow you to have a clear vision of your aim. Many times we get caught up in other people's idea of what success should look like for us, but it is important to resist this tendency and focus on how God is leading you on your path. Be reminded that everyone has their own unique journey, so don't get stuck comparing your path with that of another.

Common practice is to focus on money, power, and popularity when thinking about success. If you're starting a business or beginning to create a presence on social media, the questions arise around how well you're doing as it relates to financial gains, or how much influence you have in your industry. Don't fall prey to allowing those factors to determine your sense of accomplishment and success.

Try this exercise: Define what success means to you without referring to profit, influence, or popularity. It may not come naturally to you, but when you can do this exercise you will be able to release yourself from the societal standard for success. When we let go of those types of pressures we become free to flow as we feel led, instead of stressed out about impressing our onlookers.

There are three main factors that need to be considered when aiming for success: your attitude, your mental space, your surroundings, and your accountability.

1.  *Attitude*

Your mindset will determine how your success story plays out. Therefore, take some time to figure out how you will approach the venture you are embarking on. I imagine you have many positive thoughts about your undertaking, as well as feelings of excitement and anticipation. At the same time, it's also natural for you to have feelings of fear, uncertainty, and self-doubt. Having mixed emotions throughout the journey can be expected, but work hard on managing your outlook at all times.

Attitude can be defined as a settled way of thinking or feeling about someone or something, typically one that is reflected in a person's behaviour. Attitudes begin in our thinking and make their way to our behaviours. So imagine when a person's thinking towards their goals is negative. If they are fed up, tired, and frustrated with how things are going, eventually those negative thoughts will make their way to their behaviours. The choices they make will reveal that their outlook is unpleasant, which will affect how they are perceived. Having a pleasant attitude will impact your ability to reach your goal successfully. Remember that your purpose is not self-focused; it must positively impact the world around you. As such, if your attitude is poor, then others will be turned off and you may miss out on an opportunity to share what you have to offer.

Sometimes we think that our internal thoughts are just between us and God, but the truth is verbal communication is only a part of the way we share our thoughts with others. People can pick up on all the non-verbal cues we give off, and our negative outlook will be evident to those we interact with.

Manage the thoughts you have. Remember to daily renew your mind and fill it with the truth of God. Make it a habit to repeat those truths out loud in order to counteract all the negativity the enemy sends your way. Managing your attitude

> Manage the thoughts you have, remember to daily renew your mind, and fill it up with the truth of God.

will allow you to have more pleasant interactions with others. I always say that we should consider the taste we are leaving behind after we've interacted with someone. Will there be a sour after-taste from being in your presence or will it be a sweet one, leaving people wanting more?

2.  *Mental Space*

Being at a healthy place mentally goes hand in hand with having a positive attitude towards your ambitions. Having a healthy outlook on your life isn't something that always comes naturally. It requires intentionality, hard work, and certain key steps within your life plan.

**Maintaining a Healthy Mind and Outlook**

*Self-Awareness:*

Who are you and what are you all about? What are the things that make you tick and motivate you to keep going forward? What are the things that have held you back in life and what are the things that are currently slowing you down? How are you doing today? How have you been doing up until today?

Those are just a few of the questions you can ask yourself to check up on your emotions. It may seem silly to consider, but the truth is that the idea of self-awareness is very key to achieving success in life. How can you be sure that the goals you are striving for have originated from your spirit as opposed to having been imposed by society, family, or your community?

On our own, our heart's desires will be selfish and sinful at the core. It may seem hard to believe, but we are reminded of what comes out of our hearts in Matthew 15:19. We are also reminded in Jeremiah 17:9 that the heart of man is deceitful above all things and cannot be understood. When we submit our hearts to the Lord, He will plant His desires inside our hearts and turn our hearts from stone to flesh (Ezekiel 11:19). But how can you honestly turn your heart to God if you don't take the time to understand who you are? Once we have honestly examined ourselves, we will acknowledge the deficiencies we have and run to God, recognizing how desperately we need Him.

It's hard to think about understanding ourselves completely without letting the Creator show us the way. True self-awareness occurs when we allow the Holy Spirit to show us what needs our attention. When we are lonely, hurt, or feeling inadequate, there are things we naturally do to compensate for these feelings; but it is

God who has the solutions to all our issues. If we are going to succeed, we need to be honest about what's happening on the inside so that God can lead us to the solutions we need to move forward in a healthy way.

*Deal with issues as they arrive*

How many times have you realized that you had a problem that needed addressing, but you didn't have the time, energy, or resources to deal with it at the time? Oftentimes, when we delay it causes the problem to fester and eventually become bigger and harder to deal with in the end.

As we discussed in Chapter 8, roadblocks come in all shapes and sizes, and they are always difficult to face. If you plan to navigate around them successfully, you must be willing to address them as they arise and avoid sweeping them under the rug.

A long and overflowing list of issues that need your attention will be detrimental to your mental health. It will increase your stress and anxiety, and, in time, could lead to feelings of distress, confusion, and depression. Don't let something that is an anthill slowly form into a mountain; deal with issues as soon as possible. You'll be thankful you did after it's been addressed.

Waiting to deal with a problem isn't going to make it go away, so take a moment to jot down ideas on how you could deal with the issue and make a plan of action towards resolution. Some steps will need to be executed immediately; others can be set for a later date. The important thing is to have a plan in place to deal with each issue.

*Celebrate achievements*

People often get themselves stuck in a vortex where their only focus is the grand finale—the published book, their goal weight, etcetera. Don't allow yourself to get sucked into that mindset. What seems like your final destination today is just one stop on your life map. Once you reach it, you'll have another destination that you desire to reach.

Our goals take time to be reached, so you'll need motivation along the way to keep going. Recognize the baby steps you have taken towards your immediate goal and schedule moments to celebrate the small achievements. Stopping to celebrate smaller achievements will give you a sense of momentum as you move forward.  If your goal is to save $5,000 and you make a point to celebrate every time you see another $500 in your savings account, you will foster the feeling of "I can do this! Look at all the steps I've made thus far. My next mini goal is $500, I can do that!"

Celebrating along the way helps you remember that what you are doing is attainable as long as you stick with it. Stopping to cheer yourself on can take the form of giving yourself a treat, sharing with those on your support team, or giving yourself a day off. Whatever style you choose doesn't matter, as long as it allows you to keep moving forward.

*Self-Care*

Jesus was asked in the New Testament which commandment is the greatest. His response was "Love the Lord your God with all your heart, all your soul, all your mind and all your strength. The second is this: Love your neighbour as yourself" (Mark 12:29-31). That goes along with the golden rule that many of us were taught growing up —treat others as you would like to be treated. But how will we know how to treat others well if we don't treat ourselves well? Doing nice things because we've been told to isn't really following the instructions of Christ in the New Testament, since we are encouraged to love others as we love ourselves. Therefore, we need to consider how we treat ourselves, and ask God how to love ourselves so that we can love others. We should learn how to treat others well as we learn how to treat ourselves well.

Self-care is accomplished when a person actively treats themselves well and considers how they are feeling and what they need in order to be in a healthy place, mentally, physically, emotionally, and spiritually. Proper self-care cannot be accomplished without the leading of the Holy Spirit. It involves becoming mindful and intentional about healthy choices, surrounding ourselves with healthy people, and breaking habits that keep us stuck in an unhealthy place.

One of the best examples of self-care I've heard was from a friend Marjorie who shared that she thinks of self-care and the necessity for it as the oxygen mask on an airplane that you are instructed to put on yourself first before trying to help those around you. Many times as parents we put the care of our children first, which is natural.

However, if you are a parent and you aren't making time for good self-care, then your family actually gets you at your worst, not at your best.

3. *Surroundings*

Your surroundings will determine your level of success. If you are in an environment where people don't typically succeed and there is more discouragement than encouragement, then your attempts to excel will be stifled. That doesn't mean that if you come from, or are currently in, an environment that is not very progressive there is no hope for you to be successful. Rather it means that you need to work diligently at changing your surroundings. If you are in a job where people are very negative and there isn't room for your creative mind, it doesn't mean that you need to quit your job today, it just means that you need to begin to seek out ways to change your surroundings. Perhaps you need to put up encouraging quotes and scriptures in your work space that will uplift your spirit and encourage you to stay motivated in your pursuits.

Think about the people who currently make up your surroundings, these are your influencers and so it is important that you regularly examine how these influencers are contributing to your surroundings. Are they helping to make your surroundings a healthy place for your ambitions, or are they toxic?

It may be hard to admit, but not everyone that is currently in your circle of influence is there for your good. The word says that the enemy comes to seek, kill, and destroy, and he will sometimes use the people who are in close proximity to you to cause you the most harm and hurt you the deepest. When we come to this realization, we will be in a better position to decide who to keep close and who to create more distance from.

Toxic people are people who make us feel unpleasant once we've left their presence. They are gifted in the art of tearing down; they have a knack for pointing out what's wrong in everything and everyone, and leave you feeling worn out after spending time with them. Instead of feeling good about yourself, you are left feeling poorly about yourself and the world around you after spending time with these kinds of people. There are some people in this category who are well aware of their flaws; however, many of the toxic people we find ourselves surrounded by aren't aware of their nature, which makes it even harder to be around them.

It isn't your responsibility to change people. Your responsibility is to fulfill your purpose to the best of your ability. Therefore, when dealing with toxic and unhealthy people in your life, don't try to change them, just focus on changing your surroundings and their influence over you. Even if circumstances are such that you can't get away from the toxic people in your life (for example, you're married to them, have to work with them, or you're related to them), ask God to show you how to protect yourself from their negativity.

> Surround yourself with people who are going to facilitate your growth.

Surround yourself with people who are going to facilitate your growth. Find the people who encourage you and spend time with them. Find successful people and spend time with them. Proverbs 27:17 says that iron sharpens iron, so surround yourself with people who are willing to sharpen you. It isn't enough to avoid toxic people; you must also know how to create the type of surrounding that will be most helpful for your growth and success.

## 4. Accountability

Accountability is another word used to define responsibility and the fact that you are held liable when what you are responsible for is or isn't done. Accountability involves putting measures in place that will help you give an account for what was or wasn't done. If you are planning for success, then you need to plan to be held accountable for what you are committing to do.

No one is perfect and we all get into a place where we come up short on our commitments, so it's imperative that there is a plan in place for when that happens. If you commit to writing a blog a week and you are three weeks behind, you will need measures in place to ensure that you are held accountable. In order for you to succeed, you must have a way to chart your progress. You will need a system to help keep you on track with your progress because without one you will likely not realize that dream.

Tracking your progress involves writing your goal down and keeping yourself on track with what needs to get done. You can have an accountability partner who checks in with you or who you check in with on a regular basis. You could publicly put yourself on blast on social media so your circle is made to anticipate your progress. Or you could put reminders in your calendar, electronically or manually.

There are countless accountability tracking formats that you can employ. In your effort to be successful in your endeavours, you will need to explore which tracking system works best for you and put that in place as soon as you can. Remember that the completion of this goal is on you. It is your responsibility to figure out how this task is going to get done; and if you don't figure it out, it just won't get done. You will live to see others come after you and do exactly what you have been dreaming about completing while reading this book. The difference between the person who does and the person who doesn't is follow-through.

Recognize that this is *your* life and you are living out *your* dream, so don't be surprised if you're the only person who cares at times about your life and your dream. It may sound harsh, but it's a reality that we all need to face. It is important to find people who love and support you, but you must understand that they will not feel the same passion and interest in your life as you will.

There may be times when you are excited to share a new development and your supporters may surprise you by not showing the kind of enthusiasm as you would have liked or expected. In the moment it may feel upsetting, but it's important to remember that the burden and excitement you carry for your purpose is uniquely tied to you alone. In the end, others will benefit from it, but during the planning phases don't become too discouraged when you find yourself carrying your dream alone. There will be times of sharing with others around you and times of celebration where everyone is in synch, but there will also be times when you feel alone and unable to share the way you want with the ones you care about. My encouragement is that this time will eventually pass, so don't allow these alone times to stop you from pressing forward with your goal.

## Final Tips for Staying Motivated

*Visualize where you're going*

What is it going to feel like when you've actually reached your goal? What is it going to look like when you've accomplished your goal? Take the time to close your eyes and just imagine the emotions you will feel. What will the look on your face be like? How will those who support you express themselves? What will you have to say about reaching that goal?

Take the time to imagine meeting that goal every now and then, and allow yourself to build hope, faith, and excitement around your success. Don't be afraid to talk to God about it. Be bold and thank Him for walking you through to the end. Have a heart of expectancy. Just like the army of Israel did in 2 Chronicles 20:21. King Jehoshaphat sent out the choir to sing God's praises, believing that the victory would be theirs, and it was. Don't miss the opportunity to thank God for your victory and enjoy visualizing it before it all comes together.

In the movie *Chariots of Fire*, Eric Liddell's character said, "You came to see a race today. To see someone win. It happened to be me. But I want you to do more than just watch a race. I want you to take part in it. I want to compare faith to running in a race. It's hard. It requires concentration of will, energy of soul. You experience elation when the winner breaks the tape, especially if you've got a bet on it. But how long does that last? You go home. Maybe your dinner's burnt. Maybe you haven't got a job. So who am I to say, 'Believe, have faith,' in the face of life's realities? I would like to give you something more permanent, but I can only point the way. I have no formula for winning the race. Everyone runs in her own way, or his own way. And where does the power come from to see the race to its end? From within. Jesus said, 'Behold, the Kingdom of God is within you. If with all your hearts, you truly seek me, you shall ever surely find me.' If you commit yourself to the love of Christ, then that is how you run a straight race."

*Beware of jealousy and envy*

Two very toxic emotions that will continually try to creep up inside of you are jealousy and envy. Seeing what another person has as better or failing to value what you have as enough will only cause you to lose your focus. Jealousy and envy are bitter emotions. I describe these emotions as ones I can actually taste, and not just feel. They inhibit you from appreciating all the blessings you have, and, if left unchecked, they will cause you to jeopardize relationships and opportunities.

Break yourself out of the habit of comparing yourself—your talents, your opportunities, your progress, your potential—with others. Just don't do it! I know it's hard not to compare because our culture sets us up to do just that. If there are two sisters who sing, it's almost impossible to talk about their talent without comparing who is the stronger of the two.

> Seeing what another person has as better, or failing to value what you have as 'enough' will only cause you to lose your focus.

We are encouraged by secular media to look at others and put their stuff up against ours and compare. Then when we see what's naturally different, we end up feeling like we don't measure up. Every so often you might end up feeling like you're ahead, but that feeling won't last long, and it can't, because we're human and we're all different. So embrace your journey and focus solely on that. Fight hard and resist the urge to compare. You will flourish that much more once you learn the art of not comparing.

*Embrace the struggle*

One of the most popular slogans for working hard is 'no pain, no pain.' This phrase has typically been used to describe the hard work that goes into sports and physical exertion for the purpose of seeing physical results, but the same is true in many other aspects of life. Anything worth having will cost you greatly.

Starting a business, losing weight, going back to school, starting a blog, whatever the goal, you must accept the fact that it is going to cost you something to achieve it. And the level of success you achieve will be connected to the level of sweat you put in. Whether it is physical sweat, mental sweat, or just the sweat of consistently doing what needs to be done without deviating. Nothing comes without a bit of struggle. Therefore, start your journey by preparing to embrace the struggle that is coming.

Don't get too overwhelmed by the thought of the struggle. Our accomplishments have less to do with us anyway and more to do with God, regardless of how much we work. With that said, be sure to commit all the steps of your journey to the Lord. Regardless of what you are aspiring to create, without God's hand on it, it won't come to much. Psalm 127:1 says that "Unless the Lord builds the house, the builders labour in vain."

*Continually work on the areas where you need growth*

Don't be afraid to admit your flaws. We all have flaws; actually, we all have tons of them, so you fit right in with the rest of humanity. Having flaws isn't usually what blocks people from succeeding. It's the unwillingness to work on strengthening those flaws that cause people to fail. Look at areas where you've failed as opportunities to learn and grow in life experiences and wisdom. Instead of saying you have no regrets, recognize that your regrets help you to make better choices next time. Live and learn, all the while allowing God to show you how to make better choices with each new step.

Learn to play to your strengths and continually work the areas in your life that require growth. Make a commitment to yourself to keep on learning and growing into your best self. Give yourself the best that you can, you deserve it!

*Prepare for your next adventure*

As I mentioned previously, during my late teens and early twenties I used to love reading romance novels. I would come to the end of one book and begin to feel a sense of grief because my time with the characters was coming to an end. While I was enjoying my time reading, I was also filled with regret with every page I turned because I knew the end was quickly approaching.

Likewise, when we are on a journey and enjoying the process, we can begin to develop mixed feelings as we approach the end. When we've worked so diligently on our goal, and perhaps even lost ourselves in the process, it becomes sad thinking about it coming to an end. Sometimes, when people begin to feel this way, they self-sabotage or intentionally slow down in hopes of extending the enjoyable feelings they are experiencing. In order to prevent yourself from falling prey to this feeling, be sure to have a clear picture of what the next adventure will be. Perhaps you're writing a book and you've come to the end and you wonder what you'll do with yourself after you're all done. One way to look ahead would be to think about the strategy for marketing and getting the book in the hands of the people you wrote if for.

*Have Fun*

And last, but certainly not least, have fun! Make life and the journey to accomplishing your goals enjoyable and fun. Working towards attaining your ambitions in life won't be easy. It will come with its challenges and even discouragements at times, so do what you can to make the journey enjoyable. This may not always seem easy, for at times people naturally get bogged down with the responsibilities ahead of them and the list of things to be done. Hence, it is important to insert fun into your map. This may seem like a no-brainer if you're naturally a fun-loving person, but not everyone remembers to make their journey enjoyable. Some things are naturally enjoyable, but others require that you put effort into making them fun.

In closing, let us remember the words of Proverbs 19:21, "Many are the plans in a person's heart, but it is the Lord's purpose that prevails." Mapping out the course for your life cannot be done outside of submitting your will and desires to the Lord. The Holy Spirit will ultimately lead you in the way you need to go. You can walk in obedience and experience success, or you can resist and increase the level of struggle you face. Ultimately, what this verse reminds us of is that in the end only God's purpose will prevail. So I encourage you, one last time, to commit all your ways to Him and let Him lead you.

# Key Questions
Prepared for Success

1.  What does success look and feel like as it relates to your goal?

2.  How has your attitude and outlook prepared you for success?

3.  How will you celebrate your smaller accomplishments on your way to achieving your goal?

4.  What fun thing have you done on your journey to your goal?

5.  How can you make a task that needs to be completed on your map fun this week?

# Prayer

Hello God, this journey towards my goal isn't easy. Lord, please don't let me faint when I begin to feel weary. I look at all that is left to be completed and I feel overwhelmed. I doubt myself and my ability to complete this task successfully. Help me, Lord, to stop looking at myself, and help me to look to you. Help me to look to the hills to where my help comes from. My help comes from you, Lord. Show me how to pace myself for the road that lies ahead. Help me remain faithful to the call you have on my life. Help me never to forget that your call on my life is more important than my level of comfort. Help me to never stop trusting you.

In the book of Philippians Paul says, "I can do all things through Christ who strengthens me." He speaks about the ability to remain content and peaceful regardless of the place he finds himself in life. As I look at my life and my pursuits, help me to say the same prayer, Lord. Remind me daily that I have exactly what I need to be successful. When I start to shift my focus on things outside of you, I ask that you would quickly shift my focus back to you. I submit my will to you. I submit my plans to you. My future is yours. All I am and ever hope to be I lay down for you to use as you please. I stand on my faith, trusting that you are faithful to complete what you have begun in my life, in Jesus' name.

Amen

# Chapter 9: Prepared for Success

www.ingramcontent.com/pod-product-compliance
Lightning Source LLC
Chambersburg PA
CBHW071218090426
42736CB00014B/2886